Principles of Merchandising

D. Berkeley Wright, B.A., A.Inst.M.

LONDON
BUTTERWORTHS
1969

ENGLAND: BUTTERWORTH & CO (PUBLISHERS) LTD.
LONDON: 88 KINGSWAY, W.C.2.

AUSTRALIA: BUTTERWORTH & CO. (AUSTRALIA) LTD.
SYDNEY: 20 LOFTUS STREET
MELBOURNE: 343 LITTLE COLLINS STREET
BRISBANE: 240 QUEEN STREET

CANADA: BUTTERWORTH & CO. (CANADA) LTD.
TORONTO: 14 CURITY AVENUE, 16

NEW ZEALAND: BUTTERWORTH & CO. (NEW ZEALAND) LTD.
WELLINGTON: 49/51 BALLANCE STREET
AUCKLAND: 35 HIGH STREET

SOUTH AFRICA: BUTTERWORTH & CO. (SOUTH AFRICA) LTD.
DURBAN: 33/35 BEACH GROVE

©
D. B. Wright
1969

Standard Book Number: 406 79900 8

Printed in Great Britain by Northumberland Press Limited, Gateshead

To my wife, Joan Marie, God bless.

The shortest distance between people is a smile.

Foreword

Any study of store operations is complicated and therefore difficult for the new buyer or student of merchandising. Simplification of these processes provides only a superficial study of an intricate subject. There is a real need in Britain for a study in the language commonly used among retailers, for the idiom used by the trade is best understood by its members.

It is with general principles in mind that the subject was approached. In view of the shortage of entrants with advanced education, it is essential to train those we have to a higher standard in order to meet the challenge of the future. The principles of merchandising should be the main study of every buyer, assistant and supervisor.

As a graduate followed by service as a trainee manager, Departmental Manager, Staff Manager and as a buyer, the need for advanced training became apparent. Experience of these various levels of store management has helped me to form a very high regard for the position of retailing in a modern economy. Any fault in description of the techniques discussed I apologize for in advance, in the knowledge that there is an almost infinite variation in methods of buying and selling. Marketing is becoming more complicated; my object here is to elucidate basic principles developed by successive store managements, both in the field of chain and departmental store organizations.

I would like to thank those who have assisted in the preparation of this study and especially the students on the Courses of Retail Management Principles, who, since 1959 have year by year helped to add meaning to the subject and the conviction that merchandising should be studied and does lead to practical results. My thanks are also extended to Mr. T. Ellis-Jones, B.Sc., who, as Head of Commerce Department, Swansea College of Technology, provided the opportunity to teach these principles. Thanks go to my brother, John T. Wright, M.A., who spent valuable time reading the manuscript and contributed much towards the final layout.

Now as Lecturer in Marketing at Sheffield College of Technology, these principles have provided some practical material for marketing students.

D.B.W.
Sheffield, 1968

Contents

1.0

The Nature of the
Merchandising Function

1.1 Merchandising is the main function of the retailer and
never ceases to exercise the ingenuity and attention of those
engaged in buying and selling. Retail distribution is a great
industry, employing almost three million individuals. For the
purposes of this study, we shall consider the following
categories:
  The Unit Shop
  The Chain Store
  The Department Store
  The Speciality Chain
  The Mail Order House
  The Co-operative Societies
  As the principles are basic to them all we shall not discuss
each category separately, but rather refer to each one as the
principles apply.
  The search for the most apt definition of the merchandising
function leads to the study of profit. One possible definition,
*The process of distribution by which a profit is made by holding
stock and by making sales*, is adequate, but must be qualified
in the sense that the stock must be the right stock. Only the
right stock enables sales to be made and so merchandising as
a study must be an analysis of this concept. The word profit,
too, has many meanings. To Adam Smith it meant rent for
land, wages for labour, a return on stock and interest on capital.
But to the retailer the meaning of profit is determined by one
simple and precise object and that is to make a return on
investment sufficient to cover expenses and provide a reward
for risking capital, but of a size that will enable him to remain
highly competitive and thus promote goodwill.

1.2 The first principle of merchandising is the process of

getting, maintaining and balancing stock, and this must be the *right stock*. This is commonly termed the 'five rights':

The right merchandise—quality
The right quantity
The right place
The right time
The right price

These factors, quality, quantity, place, time and price, when perfectly equated enable the retailer to maximize profit on the minimum investment. If any one, or more, of these is misjudged, a loss of profit is made.

The relative importance of each of the 'five rights' may be argued. Before analysing each it is necessary to note the importance of having a retailing policy. The policy in a unit shop is decided and carried out by the entrepreneur. In the larger unit, the policy is decided and communicated by the Board of Directors. The policy determined for the various units must affect the precedent given to these five factors and we shall examine this problem later. Policy and decisions come from the Directorate and merchandising begins here. See diagrams 1.2A and 1.2B.

1.3   TIMING OF OPERATIONS

First, we must examine the 'right time', for however correct a retailer is in merchandising in terms of quality, quantity, place, and price, stock must arrive and be promoted at the right time. Christmas crackers are poor investments in summer, and fireworks should not be accepted into stock on, or after November 6. Winter coats in the south are slow sellers after November. In foods, the timing is even more critical, especially when keeping life is brief. Craze merchandise has a highly critical timing factor. In fact, every part of the retailing process evolves around this timing factor. If manufacturers were able to supply all merchandise on request, problems of timing would disappear and better balanced stocks would lead to higher profits and lower prices. This theoretical elasticity, in fact, rarely ever exists in the market except in basic lines and these consist of underwear or similar merchandise.

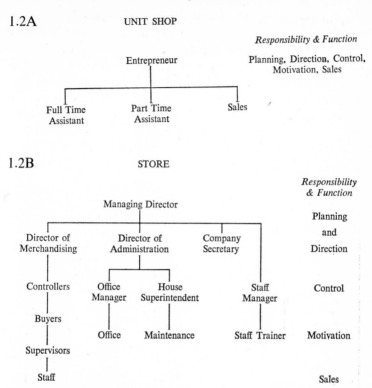

1.2A UNIT SHOP

Responsibility & Function

Entrepreneur — Planning, Direction, Control, Motivation, Sales

Full Time Assistant | Part Time Assistant | Sales

1.2B STORE

Responsibility & Function

Managing Director

Director of Merchandising | Director of Administration | Company Secretary — Planning and Direction

Controllers | Office Manager | House Superintendent | Staff Manager — Control

Buyers

Office | Maintenance | Staff Trainer — Motivation

Supervisors

Staff — Sales

N.B. Each individual store would have a line and function graph unique and tailored to suit its growth and type of organization.

1.4 STRATEGY OF PLACE

Allied to the problem of time we must now look at the 'right place'. Merchandise must be in the right part of the store, and one department should lead logically to the next. Each customer with a need or reason for making a purchase must be led naturally from one point of sale to another. Within the chain stores, place has a wider significance. Stock must be sent to the right branch and can be transferred across country, if for any reason local sales fall off. Thus heavy outerwear has a longer season in Edinburgh and chains can transfer stock there from their more southerly regions at the end of the season in order to minimize stock holding. The retailer must receive stock in anticipation of demand, but it must be displayed and promoted in the best position within the store in order to create *impulse* on the part of the customer. Customer flow can be used to take the customer past fixtures and displays that are made specially attractive with new merchandise or highly seasonal lines. The flow can also be adapted to take customers past or into parts of the layout seldom used, by easing access and diverting the flow. To get the timing and the place in the correct relationship, deliveries from manufacturers must be scheduled to arrive before the relative demand peak occurs.

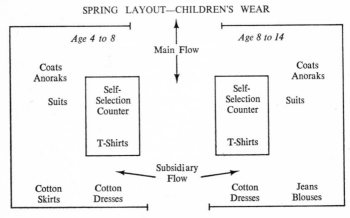

SPRING LAYOUT—CHILDREN'S WEAR

Main Promotional Features

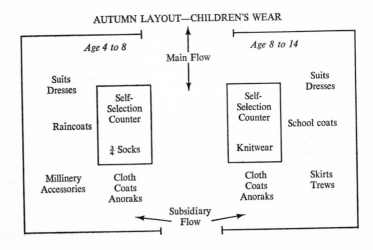

AUTUMN LAYOUT—CHILDREN'S WEAR

1.5 QUANTITY CONTROL

The 'right quantity' is another very important factor, for to any new buyer the problem of overbuying overshadows the need to retain purchasing power to deploy on lines which suddenly catch the public's imagination. High risks must be taken, but on well selected lines only. The right quantity in a Department Store depends largely on the competitive merits of each line bought. In addition the individuality of the customer must be recognized and catered for, otherwise the competitive prices of cheaper shops will have greater appeal. The Chain Store can stock a smaller variety of basic lines in great depth, but these are cut to a price and have limited style and colour appeal. Here the large quantities present a problem of selection and distribution. Production from entire factories is channelled into single organizations enabling the quantity stocked to be cut to, say, a four-week supply in relation to sales during the off-peak season and rising to a stock of 6-7 weeks prior to a peak period. In all retail units the aim should be to sell out of any line with a fashion or seasonal element. First sales on any hundred items bought in are easy, but the last are progressively difficult. The final profit on these items, however, depends on selling the last ten. Any reduction, or mark-down, reduces the overall profit on the hundred items. Where a group store can transfer the last ten, either north, or south, a more vigorous policy of merchandising can be adopted because the risks are less. (*See* Examples on pages 13-14.)

1.6 QUALITY CONTROL

The 'right quality' may be defined as *the art of expression of the merchandiser*, or the outward and visible signs of *store policy*. The merchandising objectives are decided by the Board of Directors, and the policy is interpreted by the buyer or merchandiser. The level of quality known by the customer, presented in displays, advertising, and featured on counters, rails or more exclusive types of fixtures and fittings, really portray the class of trade determined by the Board. Exclusive merchandise, of high quality manufacture, displayed individually to emphasize exclusiveness, that is accompanied by expensive fixtures and fittings and atmosphere and created by immaculate staff with personality, all determine the cus-

tomer's income group or, in broad terms, the class of trade.
Consideration of high-, medium-, or low-income groups determine these divisions, but also present further problems.
Demand for high quality is yielding to the pressures of lower
quality at cheaper prices. Class, when applied to trade, has
little relation to social class as this term is generally applied.
Class relates to the income group, depending on the ability to
pay and to determine quality and value. Where self-service and
self-selection have been adapted for reasons of efficiency,
general acceptance of these principles has cut across the older
patterns. As no store can woo every customer, specialization is
essential and competition stimulates efficiency and limits profits.

1.7   PRICE CONSIDERATION

There exists a very close relation between quality and price.
The 'right price' is that which clears a line completely, giving
a margin of profit, but at the same time provides the customer
with a value line, retaining her goodwill so that she will feel
that her decision to buy was right and was made at the right
time in the right store.

1.8   MERCHANDISING POLICY

Before we can analyse merchandising, we must know the
company policy, in order to be able to plan in harmony with
all units within the group, or departments within a store. Since
the early 1950's planning and merchandising techniques have
been made more efficient. More is now invested in the more
profitable spheres, less in slower ranges. The fusion of the
merchant and the accountant has been the most important
post-war development. Instinct and experience based on hard
facts and figures underpin all operations in our field and it is
from this point that we shall proceed to examine merchandising.

Merchandising, then, is the main theme within every store
organization. The policy is determined not by the individual
demand and need, but by the class of trade determined by the
Directors. The general principles of the trading policy should
be applied in all units of the organization. Thus the level of
trading is predetermined and depends on the expense factor,
and this determines the type of fixtures, the rate of planned

turnover required and therefore the purchasing power and the range, assortment and depth of stock to be allowed. This will lead us to analyse statistics in regard to the rate of stockturn, stock levels, the expense problems and the relative value of space in terms of square feet or £'s per linear foot. The management team are therefore responsible for analysing and controlling the retail unit.

Convention partly determines the siting and position of many of the departments within British retail units, but common sense has played a very large part. Self-selection is used on ground floor sites, but since men tend to be embarrassed when shopping, they are catered for near main entrances. Impulse goods are strategically placed, i.e. cigarettes and confectionery near cash desks in food stores. Customer flow and applied psychology must be studied to determine the right classification and siting of departments. The policy determined by the Directors will then be seen to have decided the order of priorities concerning the 'Five Rights'. If aimed at the higher income groups, then timing, quality and smaller quantities would be more important than price and place. To a group or chain, aimed at the lower income groups, quantity at a lower price, at the right time would take precedence over quality and place.

Merchandising, then, is the function that is exercised by the executive in providing stock to achieve the objectives and aims of the Company, evaluating these factors in their correct order of priority appropriate to marketing conditions and the customers they serve.

1.9 NEED FOR RESEARCH

The extensive use of consumer organizations by the public emphasizes the need for retail to play a greater part in consumer research. Manufacturers through agencies and Nielsen organizations use attitude tests, surveys, consumer panels and town tests for their product development and here lies the future for an analytical approach to retail management. This must augment the analysis of past sales records and merchandising data.

As merchandising techniques must in the main be internal, they tend to be introspective. Retail needs must be determined externally and here lies a vast field of survey work in customer attitude tests.

1.10 SYNDICATE PROBLEMS

THE NATURE OF THE MERCHANDISING FUNCTION

1. What factors determine the class of trade of a store?

2. Discuss the problems of policy making with regard to class of trade, type of store and level of trading.

3. 'Records are essential in order to operate efficiently.' Discuss the necessary records required to run a medium sized department.

4. Merchandising depends on 'timing'. Discuss this in relation to a unit shop, a chain store, a department store.

5. You are appointed manager of a run-down department in a store. What merchandising principles would you use and how would you adapt them?

6. 'Quality reflects policy.' Discuss this in relation to a chain store and a department store.

7. What information would you require before introducing a new line? How would you proceed to collect this information?

8. Is merchandising a human science or the art of intelligent estimation, or a combination of these two?

9. Planning is essential to the success of any business. What plans are essential for successful merchandising?

10. What type of stores are apparent in retailing today? Define the position of retailing in a national economy.

2.0

Price Planning

2.1   The selling price of every item in a retail unit has a direct relation to the cost price. To simplify this study we will observe this terminology throughout: *selling price is our price to the customer; cost price is the price that retail must pay to the supplier.*

2.2   Adam Smith, the recognized father of classical economic theory, studied the factors of production and from his examination of land, labour, stock and capital, assumed that price was the balancing factor between demand and supply. As mass production has narrowed the assortment and selection, the supply problem becomes more complicated. New commodities are introduced, to widen selection, and offset the narrower mass market. The new supplier becomes over-committed and ranges in retail become broken and incomplete. Specialization is the true answer in smaller, more exclusive classifications. In retail terms, then, price must be low enough to satisfy the customer, on the one hand, but it must be high enough to cover:
  (1) The cost of supply
  (2) A proportion of the overheads
  (3) Possible price reductions
  (4) A profit

2.3   THE COST OF SUPPLY
  During the immediate post-war period, when goods were mainly in short supply, the cost factor was not as important as the availability factor. Gradually during the 1950's supply price engaged the buyer's attention so that in the 1960's the problem of selection from an increasing range has become the task of prime importance. As competition intensifies the supply price becomes relatively more important. The search for the most competitive cost price now takes the buyer into the

supplier's factory to gauge its size, capacity, degree of mechanization, and its relative efficiency as regards the other competitors in the same field of merchandise. There is now a growing need for buyers to look further afield for new suppliers and specialists and this is as important as the need to renegotiate better discount rates.

The days of price fixing are now part of the past, so that a price fixed by each retailer in an area is no longer possible. Only suggested retail prices may be quoted. Where competition may be successfully countered is in the range of merchandise specially wrapped or packed for a store. This method is effective when backed by a reputable firm of retailers, where quality is more highly regarded than price. Now that a retailer cannot shelter behind price maintenance, we may now analyse alternative policies:

(1) To negotiate new discount terms on normal cost price.

(2) To use more own-brand lines.

(3) To use suggested retail prices, hoping that competitors will follow suit.

(4) To merchandise more lines which are exclusively confined to you.

(5) To use highly competitive cost and selling prices on basics, thus enabling a loss leader scheme to be operated in any department.

This last operation we shall return to later, at length. It is so vital a part of modern merchandising techniques that it will form an important part of our study.

2.4   A PROPORTION OF THE OVERHEADS

Store overheads can only be covered in the mark-up operation in every department. The definition of a department within a store is the *smallest division against which overheads can be charged*. As mark-up is never, or should never be a fixed increase on cost for each items, we cannot express mark-up as fixed $x\%$ on cost. We can plan an average mark-up in terms of different groups of items, but pricing must be flexible. Low mark-up should be the aim of loss leader lines, to bring more customers into the store. Competitive mark-up should be achieved on basic items, and these policies can be balanced by a higher mark-up on fashion, or non-basic items.

By specializing in a few selected lines an above average mark-up may be made. Customers in general are slow to analyse relative values of non-food lines and therefore tend to rely on the experiences of neighbours and friends to a larger extent.

The policy of the store is normally set out in general terms with regard to mark-up. Within a department the mark-up target is planned so that on average the department makes its proper contribution to overheads. This must be low enough to be highly competitive, yet high enough to cover staff costs, rental, rates, heating, lighting and a fair proportion of administrative costs.

2.5   POSSIBLE PRICE REDUCTIONS

The reward to investing capital and for taking risks is profit. The retailer takes less risk with basic stock and a higher degree of risk the more one introduces a fashion or seasonal element. There is the risk that styles, colours, sizes, quality, timing, or price may have been wrongly calculated in the pre-season planning process. This tends to produce residual stocks which usually find a shelf in the stockroom. Capital that is always needed in some other section is therefore lying idle and unproductive. During this idle period, stock loses its freshness and appeal and finally is marked down at the end of the season. Thus the over-buy is turned into cash, eventually, but at a lower price than its original price. The mark-up must be high enough initially to cover this mark-down.

2.6   PROFIT

During any continuous battle casualties are bound to occur and we have seen how allowance is made for these. Each item bears a price contributing towards profit, but during the continuous buying and selling process, some items are marked down and may not necessarily fulfil this obligation. Without an overall profit, any store would cease to function, so profit must always be the aim of the organization.

It is an axiom in retailing that the higher the volume of sales the easier it is to run a department. Less slow stock is created and this tends to be easy to mark-down and dispose of. Stock marked down during the season due to soiling represents a small percentage inversely proportionate to the volume of

sales. Alternatively, a low volume of sales limits the clearance
of ranges either during the Sale period, or as a continual
policy during each season. Thus the larger the volume of sales
then the smaller is the difference between initial mark-up and
average mark-up.

Having now examined the field of merchandising in a very
general way, we must analyse in the next chapters various
aspects in detail.

2.7   SYNDICATE PROBLEMS

PRICE PLANNING

1. What factors determine retail price?

2. 'Price is the equation of supply and demand.' Discuss the
various factors in retailing that tend to upset the equilibrium.

3. 'Price is the difference between profit and loss.' Define the
problems and the fallacies of this statement.

4. Does the pricing of basic stock differ from the pricing
of non-basic stock? Why should this be part of a store's policy?

5. 'Price reflects the efficiency of the buyer of a department.'
Should we consider the efficiency of manufacturer or wholesaler?

6. 'In the wake of low prices comes poor quality.' How can
a buyer steer between these two?

7. What expense must be considered in planning a pricing
policy?

8. If a new manager is appointed, what steps could he take
if the general level of prices were found to be (*a*) Too high,
(*b*) Too low?

9. What effects has price on the class of trade and on the
volume of trade? How can these effects be influenced?

10. Discuss the relative merits of pricing individual items,
or using a single price ticket for a range of items.

3.0

Mark-up

3.1 By definition mark-up is the *difference between cost price and selling price.*

COST + TAX + MARK-UP = RETAIL PRICE

Tax should be treated as a separate item on which profit is never made. Mark-up is the basic addition to the cost price.

The complicating factor in the study of mark-up is time. The inevitable time-lapse between receiving and marking an item and putting it into stock and the precise moment of selling the item to the customer varies with each line. The newsagent, for example, receives his papers and sells out at a fixed price. This is the simplest type of mark-up operation. With fashion buying, the coats received today may not sell for many weeks. Items which arrive regularly and sell very quickly must realize their initial selling price, requiring no reductions whatsoever. In the second category of merchandise, the initial mark-up, giving the selling price, may have to be adjusted downwards until the goods sell. It can be seen from the following examples that the initial mark-up is higher than the average mark-up achieved.

EXAMPLE 3.1A   On purchase of 100 shirts

Cost	Retail	Profit
Each shirt, 20/-	29/6	9/6
100 shirts £100	£147. 10. 0.	£47. 10. 0.

This represents 47·5 per cent on cost or 32·2 per cent on selling.

EXAMPLE 3.1B   As in the example above, we assume that the last ten shirts were reduced to 15/- to clear all stocks, the effect on profit now becomes:

Cost	*Retail*	*Profit*
90 shirts @ 20/-, £90	£132. 15. 0.	£42. 15. 0.
10 shirts @ 20/-, £10	£7. 10. 0.	−£2. 10. 0.
Total £100	£140. 5. 0.	£40. 5. 0.

Representing 40·2 per cent on cost or 28·7 per cent on selling.

With the initial mark-up at 32·2 per cent on selling, the reduction of a tenth of the consignment to half price results in an average mark-up of 28·7 per cent or a 3·5 per cent reduction in gross profit.

Terminology must again be considered, since in practice mark-up percentage is normally expressed as a percentage on *selling*, rather than on cost. This problem may also be presented in terms of proportional profits against cost:

EXAMPLE 3.1C

Cost	*Selling*	*Profit*
25/-	37/6	12/6

Mark-up = 12/6

$$\text{Mark-up \%} \quad \frac{12/6}{25/-} \; = \; 50\% \; = \; \tfrac{1}{2} \text{ of cost}$$

$$\frac{12/6}{37/6} \; = \; 33\cdot3\% \; = \; \tfrac{1}{3} \text{ of selling}$$

Fractionally we can always add one to the denominator to work the fraction of selling, given the fraction of cost, e.g.

$$\tfrac{1}{2} \; \frac{\text{(profit)}}{\text{(cost)}} \; = \tfrac{1}{3} \; \frac{\text{(profit)}}{\text{(selling)}} \quad : \quad \tfrac{1}{4} \; \frac{\text{(profit)}}{\text{(cost)}} \; = \tfrac{1}{5} \; \frac{\text{(profit)}}{\text{(selling)}}$$

The difference between cost and selling prices has been expressed as the mark-up or gross profit, but this must be enough to cover overheads and expenses. Thus it can be seen that in planning mark-up it is essential to consider average mark-up rather than initial mark-up. Therefore we must plan an initial mark-up high enough to realize the average mark-up required.

In order to plan an initial mark-up that would be high enough to cover all expense factors, we must consider the expenses incurred in buying, the profit margin required to sustain the department or store, the possibility of stock loss and mark-downs and discount, and any further cost item such as alteration charges and could be expressed in the following equation:

Initial Mark-up = (Expenses + Profits + Alteration charges — Discounts + Mark-downs + Stock shortages + Employee discounts) ÷ (Sales + Mark-downs + Shortages + Employees discounts.)

In general terms, then, we must first estimate sales, and then calculate reductions and expenses. We must then calculate the Net profit margin required. By using the equation above, the mark-up percentage can be calculated:

> Estimated Sales £100,000 per year
> Expenses £30,000   Reductions £10,000
> Profit Target £5,000 or 5%
> Mark-up = £30,000 + £10,000 + £5,000
> Add Expenses £10,000 + £100,000 = £110,000
> Mark-up percentage = $\dfrac{45,000}{110,000}$ = 40·9%

3.2   Next we must look at the problem of mark-up in relation to competition. It is obvious that mark-up will affect the volume of sales, for in a highly competitive range of merchandise, a store may forego the full profit in order to be highly competitive and attract more custom, as may be illustrated in the following equations:

> Average mark-up 33·3% on £1,500 sales = £500 profit
> Average mark-up 25% on £2,000 sales = £500 profit

3.3   To remain highly competitive with a lower, and therefore a more attractive price structure, sales must be increased, in this example by £500, or a 33·3 per cent increase in order to achieve the same profit margin. In a department store cutting prices in one department can affect other departments, but the overall increase in the volume of sales must be high to justify a cut, due to the high expenses-costs involved. The effect among several departments is difficult to attribute to increased customer flow, due to the factors that are complex and interdependent in each department. We shall consider the effects of loss-leader merchandising in non-food departments later, but in a limited field this can lead to an increase in customer flow and can therefore be applied to many departments, and the effect of reductions in average mark-up must be considered. Since the winds of change are blowing more and more strongly down the High Streets of Britain today, no buyer can afford to ignore the effect of mark-up on customer flow. The customer finds more goods from which to select and competition grows week by week, so that the need to attract and serve becomes more important. The mechanism of market reaction is extremely intricate but it must be carefully studied and the results should produce action.

3.4   Where the risk of mark-down, breakage, deterioration, theft or obsolescence is inordinately high, then it is normal practice to make a higher than normal mark-up. On special lines, such as high cost or exclusive lines, a higher than normal mark-up can be made.

Where basic merchandise only is involved, and mark-downs are small, the mark-up may be below average. This may also occur when handling is light, where no alterations are involved, and a high degree of competition may be met, or where opposition must be countered.

There is more art than science in deciding the right price, but the basic principle must be to equate profitability with goodwill and repeat business. Mark-up must produce an increasing volume of sales. The psychology of fast selling lines creates satisfaction and wins the approbation of the customers, and impresses upon them the values offered within the store.

3.5   SYNDICATE PROBLEMS

MARK-UP

1. 'The retailers profit is the difference between cost and selling.' Discuss the fallacies of this statement.

2. What items of expense in a department should be considered when planning mark-up?

3. 'Mark-up at cost differs from mark-up at selling.' Why is this? What are the relative merits of each system?

4. What factors must be considered in planning mark-up?

5. What difference appears between initial mark-up and the average mark-up?

6. What difference does volume of trade make on the initial and the average mark-up?

7. 'Mark-up varies between types of stock.' Categorize the types of stock and detail the average mark-up that might be planned for each type.

8. 'The pricing of merchandise is an art, not a science.' Discuss.

9. How can a new buyer improve on the average mark-up whilst he increases the volume of sales and improves goodwill?

10. 'Competitive strength is the essential factor in a business.' Discuss this in relation to basic and non-basic and mixed sections.

4.0

Price Lining

4.1 As we have seen in the previous studies, cost price plus mark-up equals the selling price. Cost price is the result of the cost of the factors of production and is reflected in the cost of the items supplied. Each cost price may vary a copper or two, and the selling price is made by the buyer. The buyer, or retailer must make prices to satisfy his customers, so factors other than a mechanical percentage increase must be considered. To maintain a basic line of merchandise several sources of supply may be used, which are bought in at different supply prices. But the line requires to be sold at one price, so this must be averaged over the various cost prices. The chain stores adopt this principle and the goods are displayed under a single price ticket. The retail price must cover the prices charged by high cost, inefficient firms, as well as the lower cost firms.

Price lining has two elements:

(A) Grouping under a few selected prices

(B) Spacing the prices at well recognized intervals

(A) above illustrates the chain store principle. A line of vests, for example, may be priced at 3/11, 5/11 and 7/11. The prices at well selected intervals correlate with differences in size or quality.

In (B) above we have a slightly different set of cost factors which are gathered together under a few chosen selling prices:

Cost prices	Selling prices
50/7-54/0	79/6
54/1-57/6	85/0
57/7-60/6	89/6
60/7-64/0	95/0

The selling prices in this example are sufficiently divergent to be recognized as being of different cost, size or value. The customer is not faced with a mass of selling prices varying by pence, and with ten garments at 89/6, for example, her choice is not conditioned by the saving of a few pence. Mark-downs can be made to the -/11d. scale to differentiate:

| Normal Selling Prices | 79/6, 85/0, 89/6, 95/0 |
| Reduced Prices | 79/11, 89/11, 99/11 |

Prices of 50/2 or 49/7 we must assume, then, are not attractive and the retailer must either forego some profit, or add a few pence to make an attractive price. For the feminine mind, the 16-guinea ticket seems more attractive than that of £16 9s. 11d. To avoid a complete confusion of prices dependent on every price on every invoice, it is obvious that a store should have a simple but effective policy and price lining provides these advantages. A separate competitive price lining policy should mark low on basic merchandise and a separate price lining scheme for non-basics should maintain the average mark-up planned. The pricing policy of a store should be apparent on entering, for simplification of prices attracts customers. A clear pattern of prices is part of the store's psychology, it helps the customer to select more easily and the sales assistant to serve more efficiently since her knowledge of stock is simplified.

4.2   Very real advantages accrue over a period of years when a vigorous policy of price lining is carried through. The simple price structure educates the customer. Stock is concentrated in fewer price lines and is easier to catalogue for stock analysis. Mental processes are speeded up and service improves. Concentration leads to higher profits. With less duplication in the simpler range, stock is simplified and more profitable. Less investment is required, so that stock levels can be controlled to a finer degree.

4.3   With a policy of price lining more concentration leads also to increases in sales volume. This results from the increase in product knowledge and the new approach to merchandising. Fewer lines need be stocked, thus promoting better stock keeping. Staff can handle display more easily and can be taught to give space on the basis of allocating most space to the fastest lines. Side effects of price lining leading from simplification are the easing of the buying problem. From the customer's point of view selection in the markets becomes more direct whilst advertising and display become more effective. The simplification of displays enables the customer to select from a highly detailed conglomeration and it is now essential to help the customer to analyse, deduce and think about the massive array of merchandise now offered.

4.4   As selling becomes easier, mark-downs diminish. Stock of basic items can be held in greater depth which prevents loss of sales on these lines. Thus, more capital is released for risk merchandise or highly seasonal lines which can be promoted and sold quickly. The expense percentage becomes less with higher turnover and with simpler ranges, space is saved for the development of other sales promotions. Economics of larger scale buying may contribute to lower costs, fewer suppliers may be used so that the buyer has more time to devote to merchandise, staff, promotions and above all, customers. Additionally, higher discounts may result from bulk purchases.

Certain inherent disadvantages in price lining practice must also be pointed out. The fixed retail price has eliminated the process of haggling over each sale, and this, while being a great advantage to the organization of self-selection units, lacks appeal to many customers. The established prices tend to lack sales appeal, with its effect of regimentation. Reduction in the range of basic items may also antagonize customers. This limits the area over which price linings may be extended. These disadvantages are marginal, however, and the attendant advantages have proved highly beneficial to basic departments, such as shirts and underwear. In fashion departments, where price is not the dominant factor, price lining is less effective and a lack of variety would definitely limit customer appeal.

4.5   The most essential feature of any pricing policy must be flexibility. Competition must always be met. Thus no price should be fixed, but should be revised often in the short term, but in the long term must meet Company objectives. The price policy of any business should be fair, competitive and should reflect the image of the store.

4.6   RESALE PRICE MAINTENANCE (R.P.M.)

Price lining must be studied in more detail now that resale price maintenance has been generally attacked by the Government in an attempt to protect consumer interests through competitive retail prices. Where R.P.M. was normal practice each trade has had to apply to the Restrictive Practices Court for exemption and for example Bread, Detergents and Footwear have put a case and a ruling has been given. R.P.M. has been replaced by suggested selling prices. These reflect the general margins but the Prices and Incomes Board is now duly subjecting these margins to closer examination. Where a printed catalogue of merchandise is provided retail prices are difficult to pre-plan due to rising costs of labour, raw materials after devaluation and packing and postage costs. Short term movements in costs make some areas of price planning difficult to predict.

4.7   SYNDICATE PROBLEMS

PRICE LINING

1. Customers respond to various price levels. Discuss the psychology of this response.

2. In what area can a retailer price above, below, or at the same price as a competitor?

3. Price lining is the art of pricing in as few price lines as is practicable. What factors determine the number of prices to be used?

4. Pricing policies should reflect the image of the business. Can price lining effectively do this?

5. How can price lining increase the volume of trade?

6. Does price lining lead to better stock keeping, easier selling and as a result improved service to customers?

7. Can price lining lead to a reduction in costs?

8. If price lining simplifies, is flexibility lost, is trading up made difficult and does the buyer lose a degree of control?

9. Does a policy of price lining produce a range of popular prices?

10. Can price lining and loss leader merchandising be welded into a successful price policy? How could this be applied to (*a*) a basic range, (*b*) a non-basic range?

5.0

Stockturn

5.1 Stockturn is defined as *'the rate at which the average stock, in a given period of time, is sold and replaced'*. Calculation is made by adding to month-end stock figures and dividing the total by the number of months, giving the average stock figure. The sales for each of these months is then compiled and the total sales divided by the average stock gives the stockturn rate. The following figures exemplify the calculation:

Month	Sales	Month End Stock
Feb.	£300	£600
March	£450	£800
April	£600	£800
May	£400	£750
June	£350	£700
July	£400	£600
	£2,500	£4,250

$$\text{Average stock} = \frac{£4,250}{6} = £708$$

$$£2,500 \div £708 = 3 \cdot 5$$

Stockturn Rate is expressed as 3·5

This is the Retail Distributors Association (R.D.A.) method. A more accurate result can be achieved if the starting stock is included, and divided with the £4,250 by 7. The method above which is standard practice, does not include the month of February. But stockturn rate is based on the average stock figure and all we need is a standard yard-stick to compare all departments. Any formula based on average figures must contain mathematical inaccuracies and can only provide approximations of accuracy, but the stockturn formula is a very good rule-of-thumb method of comparison. The concept is the basis of profit making, and is therefore one of the most important principles of merchandising, If, for example, sales were eighty coats in six months and the average stock for this period was twenty coats, the stockturn rate would be 4·0. If the average stock was £100, the profit could be expressed as £20 four times, and £80 profit would accrue over six months. Whilst this is the arithmetical approach to the concept, stockturn may also be regarded as the expectation rate, or what may be expected from any given department trading at a known level and of a relative size. This, then, is a concept of known experience and of comparison, rather than a pure mathematical formula.

Stockturn is usually discussed in terms of decimal figures, i.e. 4·0 or 2·6. Calculations are either at cost or selling, each giving a different rate, but in normal practice stores work in terms of *stockturn at selling*.

5.2 STOCKTURN RATES

These vary enormously between different types of departments. Foods turn very quickly due to their short keeping life, whereas fashions turn at much slower rates. The higher mark-up on fashion compared with that on food reflects this difference, i.e. skill in salesmanship, high rent for selling area, high risk of obsolescence, and length of time between receipt and sale resulting in possible mark-downs. A department consisting only of homogeneous items should have a higher stockturn rate than a heterogeneous department with complicated ranges. Thus Millinery or Ladies Knitwear should have higher stockturn than Children's wear. This may not follow in the case of a complicated department situated close to a group of efficient suppliers or wholesalers, when stock levels can be kept relatively low. Much depends here on the buyer's skill in controlling stock levels. Buyers and management often differ in the fundamental idea of how much stock a department requires, for the pattern of selling is never static and a case can always be argued for buying more and more. The most difficult lesson a buyer must learn is when not to buy and when to sell out, or sell down, without losing customer's goodwill. During quiet periods, representatives are under pressure to push their sales, but stocks must be kept at a controlled level at all times especi-

ally during off-peak periods, or during the transition from one
main season to the next. If excess stock were to be bought
the average for this off-peak would be high and would cause
under-stocking during the next peak season, thus reducing the
stockturn rate by raising stock levels.

5.3   The study of stockturn rates has led to a development in
the classification of merchandise, the planning of purchases and
the study of stock control systems. Classification means the
division of a department into sections in order to analyse and
control the sales and stocks of each section, providing very
useful data when the peaks and off-peaks occur at different
times. Purchases must be planned so that maximum sales can
be achieved from minimum stocks. Stock is *the accumulation
of all purchases made and not yet sold*. The study of stock
control systems will be dealt with in Chapter 8, and has led to
quantitative and qualitative analysis. Quantitative analysis is
*the study of the level of stock sufficient to satisfy each cus-
tomer's needs, with none left over*. This is the study of the
speed at which stock sells and the time needed to replenish.
Three vital statistics are calculated, namely, sales, stock
and commitments. Qualitative analysis, on the other hand,
is *the study of the right stock for the customer*. The incomes
groups of the customers must be evaluated. Quality, therefore,
has a direct bearing on the composition of stock. This factor
has an influence at the rate at which stock will sell on a basis
of appeal.

5.4   The increase of stockturn rate is therefore the basis of all
store operations. We have now reached a stage when the
advantages which will accrue may be selected:
    (*a*) *Reduction in mark-downs*. This leads to a reduction
of the price of slow selling lines. If slow sellers are eliminated,
cleaner stocks result and stockturn can then be increased.
    (*b*) *Reduction in expenses*. Less merchandise needs less
space, simple fixtures and more self-selection for promotion.
Less staff are required and staff training is made easy on a
simpler range.
    (*c*) *Increase in sales*. This follows the process of simplifica-
tion. Customers are not confused, classification and self-

selection help to promote the rationalized image.

(*d*) *Increase in profit on investment.* If £1,000 is invested at $2\frac{1}{2}$ per cent the annual return is £25. If the return on £1,000 of stock were $2\frac{1}{2}$ per cent and the stockturn rate 5·0, this gives a total return of $12\frac{1}{2}$ per cent, or £125. Further advantages accrue when the purchases are controlled, for the open to buy figure remains open, special offers can be bought in or new trends can be exploited. The open to buy figure is *the amount of purchasing power a buyer can command at any time* and is normally given by the merchandising office at weekly intervals and is the actual stock held plus outstanding orders placed compared with the planned level of stock and purchases. A constantly changing stock never fails to attract, it looks smart in the current prevailing trend and gains prestige. If fewer suppliers are used, special orders are easier to obtain quickly. Service is therefore improved.

5.5   There are limitations to the extent to which we can improve stockturn. The danger of eliminating selection could lead to an over-simplification of the catalogue. Sales would be lost. In the rapid replacement process, more expenses may be incurred by the buyer, and a loss in bulk discounts may occur. More invoices of small quantities may increase the clerical and handling costs. But it is very obvious that these disadvantages are subordinate to the advantages.

5.6   To end this study of stockturn rates we shall now look at three problems which will demonstrate the usages of the concept:

PROBLEM 1. Given the average stock of a department is £25,000, stockturn rate is 3·0 the half year calculate the sales for the year.

Solution. Average stock = £25,000   Stockturn rate = 3·0
Half yearly sales = £25,000 × 3 = £75,000
Annual sales = £75,000 × 2 = £150,000

PROBLEM 2. Given the sales are £10,000 and the stockturn rate is 4·0, calculate the average monthly stock level.

Solution. Average monthly stock = 10,000 = £2,500

PROBLEM 3. Given annual sales of £25,000 and a half yearly average stock of £10,000 calculate the stockturn rate.

Solution. $\dfrac{25,000}{10,000} = 2.5$

In this example the term half yearly is superfluous.

5.7 SYNDICATE PROBLEMS

STOCKTURN

1. Is the concept of stockturn of sufficient mathematical precision to justify study, when the economy needs accurate method and technique?
2. Compare and contrast the various stockturn rates on a basic and a non-basic range.
3. Why do stockturn rates determine the profitability of departments?
4. Discuss the relationship between the concepts of stockturn and classification.
5. What advantages are to be gained from a study of stockturn?
6. Can the use of loss leader merchandising affect a department with a slow stockturn rate?
7. What effects has a reduced stockturn rate on the expense items of a department?
8. What effects has the study of stockturn rates had on stock keeping and stock control?
9. What factors should a buyer consider in order to increase the stockturn rate, lower stock levels, or higher sales volume?
10. What effect has an increase in stockturn rate on investment?

6.0

Principles of Buying

6.1 The aim of every buyer is to satisfy each customer and make a satisfactory gross profit. The several principles applied to achieve this are elaborated below.

6.2 ADMINISTRATION
The techniques of administration may be analysed under five headings:

PLANNING
Some plan must be made in the store to give overall targets. Each department then must be fitted into the combined plan, so that the figures of sales, purchases and stocks form the basis of the buyers target. The implications we shall look at in detail later.

ORGANIZATION
The buyer must apply work study in his layout of fixtures and fittings, however loosely we may use the term. To achieve any planned result, organization plays a very important part.

DIRECTION
The interpretation of policy as it is communicated to the buyer must be passed on to the staff. The problems of communication in a large store are only solved by the efficient use of buyers as interpreters. Apart from clarifying objectives, he must fit individual members of his department into their various roles. Each has a different attitude, work potential and motivation for being in the department and it is the buyer's job to fit people to their tasks in the most effective combination.

CO-ORDINATION
The line and function tasks must be made to work, and the supervisor must be fully trained and competent to delegate

tasks down the line. The training of each grade, be it senior, middle, or junior staff must be carried out individually and each trained member must then be integrated with an identifiable team.

CONTROL
The buyer must continually check and follow through the tasks delegated in order to balance performance and maintain the progress of each individual.

6.3 SELECTION AND BUYING
The buyer must have a comprehensive knowledge of his sources of supply. He must be able to discriminate between basic stocks and suppliers who are able to give speed of service.

The houses best at supplying non-basic merchandise are the specialist manufacturers, or importers. Selection from a very wide variety is generally made on the basis of profit, the highest discount rate, speed of delivery, or the supply of exclusive merchandise. Each section of a department will have a different set of problems like these, and each will require a different technique.

The interpretation of a buying plan is an important part of a buyer's job. He must understand how the figures are calculated and the implications involved. In this respect, he must have an appreciation of certain ratios. A ratio is the quantity of one size compared with a different quantity of the next size. We can think of this mathematical relationship in terms of sales of one size and the sales of a series of sizes, or in terms of the stock held, in variable quantities of a series of sizes. We could also think in terms of the ratio between colours, styles, price groups or sizes.

We must apply the principle of ratios to the study of needs. Customers enter our stores for three main reasons:
(a) *Necessities:* food, clothing, shelter. Departments involved are the Food Supermarkets, Ladies Fashion, Menswear and Childrens' departments, and Furniture, Carpets, Soft Furnishing and Hardwear departments.
(b) *Individuality:* fashion departments.
(c) *Economic developments:* plastics, man-made fibres, new inventions and design changes.

6.4   DEPARTMENTAL MANAGEMENT

Finally the buyer must apply the basic principles of management best suited to his department.

SUPERVISION

He must be able to train not only the supervisor in the department, but also ensure that training is being carried out throughout the various levels of staff. Each member should be known, the stages of promotion should be clear, product knowledge and promotional methods of merchandising should be a process which is regularly developed.

STAFF COSTS

The buyer should know the basis of the method used to calculate the percentage of wages to sales and whether the productivity of the department is average, above, or below average.

6.4A   STAFF COSTS RELATED TO SIX DAY TRADING

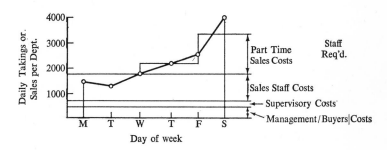

6.4B   STAFF COSTS RELATED TO FIVE DAY WEEK
(MONDAY CLOSING)

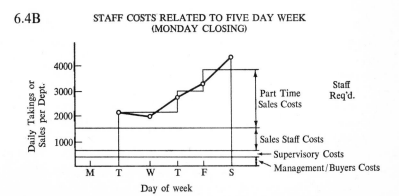

The work schedules of most departments need constant overhaul and analysis. See graphs 6.4A, B and C.

It must be noted that the expense of extra part time staff will be incurred on more days when six days trading is operated, but tends to be a lower expense on five day trading. Full time staff costs are higher, due to the day off, on a sliding weekly basis.

6.4C

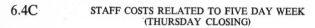

STAFF COSTS RELATED TO FIVE DAY WEEK
(THURSDAY CLOSING)

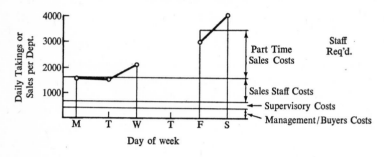

CUSTOMER RELATIONS

Is is essential to keep constant contact with demand and customer reaction. Exchanges must be examined to assess the workmanship of suppliers. Goodwill may be in jeopardy here, and the customer deserves individual attention when merchandise does not meet the standard required. Good service is essential in every business.

SALES PROMOTION

Each buyer must have a basic knowledge of how to present and ticket merchandise. Selection of items must precede their peak selling period and display principles of colour blends, attraction of shape and form must be observed.

6.5   Analysis and application of these three main principles, administration, selection and departmental management, is basic to the smooth running of any department. Customers should be satisfied now and in the future. This creates goodwill. However good the buying policy of a Company is, its ultimate success depends on the success of the staff-customer relationship. Customers only react to the degree of service rendered.

6.6 As social, economic and scientific developments create new products and new markets, other products are made obsolete. Thus the analogy of Alfred Marshall in *The Principles of Economics* that 'firms are like trees in a forest; some grow tall and flourish, whilst others succumb and die', may also apply to merchandising. A buyer must be an innovator. Progress depends on the ability to grasp new ideas, or the feeding back of new requests to designers and suppliers. The retailer is the link between the customer and the manufacturer.

6.7 A difficult aspect of this problem is the selection of the range. Specialization must take place. Stock levels must be varied to suit the precise moment in the season, and depend on the type of merchandise. Selection is the main function of the buyer. The simpler the range and the more it is concentrated and specialized, the easier it is for the customer to know and use these services. When a customer finds her favourite brand is out of stock, she feels frustrated and confused. She leaves the store discontented and annoyed. Basic lines must always be in stock. To achieve this a high degree of planning is necessary. Stock planning has reached out into all retail organizations. In the multiple organizations planning has approached a science and accurate statistics provide ratios of sales and stocks so that forward ordering is extremely accurate. In smaller units the individuals vary considerably in sophistication, education and ability. No universal merchandising system has been devised to standardize these procedures, and therefore training is essential in this field.

6.8 The decision regarding depth or breadth of stock may arise in the Boardroom or on the floor, but sectionalization of stocks gives various sets of figures so that basics may be kept in one section and non-basics in another with their individual sales, stock and commitment figures. Layout should ease the problem of customer-selection here, for this can complicate the problem of holding a simple range of stock and displaying it in logical sequence. When a customer finds one item in several parts of the same department, the time has come to simplify and rationalize the pattern of stock keeping.

6.9   SYNDICATE PROBLEMS

PRINCIPLES OF BUYING

1. What principles of Administration must a buyer apply in the daily operation of a Department?

2. Discuss the problems of supply. What methods can a buyer apply to discriminate among the infinite number of suppliers?

3. Management and Supervision are exercised in every department. Discuss the problems inherent in the efficient exercise of these functions.

4. An awareness of staff cost ratios is essential to the efficient operation of a Department. Discuss.

5. How can buyers subscribe to the success of sales promotions in the Store?

6. What effects have product knowledge and marketing knowledge on the buying plan?

7. What is meant by the term ratio as applied to stocks? How does a buyer prepare to calculate these?

8. How does a buyer analyse the problem of holding stock in depth or breadth?

9. What steps must be taken to increase sales without increasing the costs of selling?

10. What basic principles would determine the layout and the fixtures and fittings in a Department?

7.0

Techniques of Buying

7.1 The process of buying is always a highly individual, or personal problem of selection and is therefore affected by the emotional make-up of the individual. This is the variable that faces management. Strengths must be promoted and weaknesses must be reinforced. The vitality and strength of the store lies in its collective merchandising ability. The provision of accurate and really up-to-date figures of sales, stock and open-to-buy, can offset these weaknesses. In other words, collective merchandising ability can be fostered by a team of buyers who have been fully trained to appreciate statistics. Methods are only effective when fully understood and accepted. A buying plan, then, is essential in solving the problems of stock holding in depth, breadth, or in a pattern which may be a combination of both.

7.2 Having established the need for a buying plan, the next step is to examine the statistical data required and the various degrees of accuracy we may expect. Sales forecasting is the first step and is based on the known performance of the previous year. With last year's performance we must consider any factors likely to affect future trends. Bank Holiday dates vary and affect peak selling periods. Local events, festivities or large gatherings raise sales levels. New developments in the area such as large-scale industrial expansion have a predictable effect on sales. Fashion trends have an influence on sales. Delivery dates are vitally important in this case. Timing is a very important factor and chains take a short period of six to eight weeks as a basis for planning in the stores, the stock being already bought by a Head Office organization. Their basic problem is distribution to the stores. Department stores take a medium planning period of six months, the problems being related to production and delivery. Long term sales planning of periods of one to five years is carried out by management in order to plan selling space and allocation of space over a long run period.

7.3 Taking the short period first, chains are backed by central buying organizations. Their task is to assess the potential of each line, allocate finance and balance the production flow from the factory to the stock levels required. The function is divided into policy making at the executive level, subdivided into selection and distribution.

7.4 Taking a simple buying organization in a Head Office, the main tasks are the assessment of the potential of a line, the rate of flow of factory production, future potential, and the allocation of finance. This may be expressed diagrammatically:

7.4A SUGGESTED BUYING ORGANIZATION IN A HEAD OFFICE

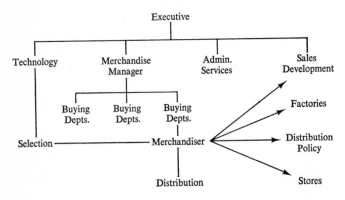

This simple method of analysing each line enables a chain to merchandise in depth with continuous control of quality and accurate timing of delivery. Thus the depth of stock can be kept low due to the continuous flow of delivery. Stockturn can be maintained at a higher rate than in a department store. Future commitments can be reduced to a six to eight week level based on the sales trend.

7.5 Turning now to the methods used in department stores, the demand for novelty lines is greater. The task of measuring forward commitments is more difficult. To simplify the wider ranges merchandised, each department is divided into sections. The technique known as classification (see below) is designed to aid stock control. The first advantage is that where seasonal fluctuations in sales occur, sales may be related more accurately to stock levels. This enables the promotion of high demand lines. It also facilitates the control of mark-downs. Whilst errors on tills tend to exaggerate the errors on each section when stock taking results are examined, the control of stock shortages is managed by sub-division into sections. Executive control is aided by classification.

7.6   Classification may be made in many ways:
1. By type of merchandise.
2. By price groups.
3. By manufacturers or source of supply.
4. By material content.
5. By a combination of one or more of these.

To remove the problem of individual taste and selection, management may take complete ranges from specialist manufacture and keep a separate selection for each of these.

The medium term buying plan normally spans a period of six months. This divides a year into a Spring-Summer season and an Autumn-Winter season. In fashion departments trends tend to follow a pattern:

Month	Level of trade	Month	Level of trade
February	Low	August	Low
March	Medium-high	September	Medium-high
April	High	October	High
May	Medium	November	Medium
June	Low	December	High
July	Medium (Sale)	January	Medium (Sale)

The March and April sales figures depend on the dating of Easter and Whitsun. The timing of the Autumn peak is early or late dependent on the falling temperature and the first signs of winter winds and cold. This affects sales of coats, knitwear and heavier clothing and as these are expensive, sales increase. Weather is the controlling influence in selling garden furniture, seeds, and garden implements.

Using the known level of sales last year and the previous year, the most accurate estimates of sales can be now calculated using performance plus knowledge of local events and national holidays. We can now consider the aspect of stockturn and examine the stock levels of previous years. This enables an estimate to be calculated monthly. First taking the starting stock or stock at the end of the previous month, deduct the estimated sales for the next month, deduct this figure from the month-end figure and the resultant figure is an estimate of the purchase figure for the month:

EXAMPLE 7.6A

Month	Estimate of sales	Purchases	Stock level	
February	£4,000	£5,000	£10,000	£9,000 starting stock
March	6,500	12,000	15,500	
April	6,000	3,500	13,000	
May	5,000	4,000	12,000	
June	4,500	2,500	10,000	
July	5,500	3,500	8,000	
	31,500	30,500	68,500	

Stockturn 2·8, per half year   Av. 11,416

The difference of £1,000 between purchases and sales for the season is accounted for in the difference of starting stock £9,000 and the ending stock of £8,000. Having estimated the sales and stock for February, the purchase figure is calculated:

$$9,000 - 4,000 = 5,000 \qquad 10,000 - 5,000 = 5,000$$

This type of buying plan must be adjusted constantly through the season and forms the target figures weekly and monthly. The nature of merchandise is different in each department, therefore the plan will be varied in every case. If the example above is taken for a department with faster selling stock, we can have identical sales with very varied purchase and stock patterns:

EXAMPLE 7.6B

Month	Estimate of sales	Purchases	Stock level	
February	£4,000	£4,000	£9,000	£9,000 starting stock
March	6,500	7,000	9,500	
April	6,000	7,000	10,500	
May	5,000	4,000	9,500	
June	4,500	3,000	8,000	
July	5,500	4,000	6,500	
	31,500	29,000	53,000	

Stockturn 3·6, per half year   Av. 8,833

The stockturn rate has increased from 2·8 in Example 7.6A to a stockturn rate of 3·6 in Example 7.6B

The plan will only work if the level of sales is achieved and the planned purchases are controlled. When substantial sales are lost, purchases must be curtailed, and where large forward commitments have been made, this may mean an adjustment period of eight to twelve weeks, dependent on speed of action taken. When orders are cancelled, the stock in the department stagnates, customers recognize old styles and sales are further depressed. Any basic stock system must be designed to prevent this stop-go. The open to buy figure in all basic merchandise must always remain open. Thus the buying operation must be divided into risk stocks and open basic stocks. Risk stock is a *new line*, a special offer, or short supply line *on which a higher than normal profit might be made in the short run.* Open basic stock includes *all the bread and butter lines*, highly competitive *which carry lower than normal mark-up.* Classification must be used to attain this object. The simple choice of Wholesaler and Manufacturer is no longer simple, but dependent on the degree of co-operation between supplier and retailer.

The buyer must learn to interpret the plan in order to balance present stocks with future commitments. He must be able to break down the sterling figure into units of stock in order to place forward orders. He must know how much to spend. He must understand the selling trends, the fastest selling merchandise and he must know the income groups of his customers.

7.7 DISCOUNTS

It is important to equate maximum customer-satisfaction with maximum profit. This is a convenient point at which to consider the problem of discount. Discounts are an extra reward for efficiency and as such are more critical as trade becomes more competitive. They fall into three main categories:

CASH DISCOUNTS

These are negotiated between retailer and supplier and include a monthly discount for prompt payment. Normally the rates are $2\frac{1}{2}$ per cent for monthly payments and $3\frac{3}{4}$ per cent for seven day payments.

TRADE DISCOUNTS

This is a discount negotiable by the retailer, over and above the normal settlement terms and an efficiency reward for buying bulk, or for specialization.

QUANTITY DISCOUNTS

These are very similar to trade discounts, but differ in that a time factor is introduced. The time factor is vital here because bulk stock is delivered at one location as a single load, thus the cost saving is passed to the retailer. The limitation is the space required to store bulk from the delivery date to the final day of sale. This may limit bulk to small companies and gives a cost advantage to larger retailers. Bulk purchases must be made in sufficient quantity to meet the production schedules of the supplier.

As most items in the market are £x cost, or £x less $2\frac{1}{2}$ per cent, or £x less 10 per cent less $2\frac{1}{2}$ per cent, a variety of cost prices exist. The larger and more efficient retailer takes advantage of this to offer the most competitive selling prices.

The ethics of buying are recognized by retailers and manufacturers. When commencing dates and completion dates are agreed and are written into an order, this constitutes a legal agreement. But owing to production difficulties, the legal agreement remains open to very loose interpretation. Early or late delivery justifies a refusal to accept the goods, but few retailers stand fast, and suppliers consequently refuse to be bound by the delivery date. The only result is timing errors in the merchandise plan which leads to overstock, slow stockturn and heavy mark-downs. There is a vital need for retailers and suppliers to co-operate on this problem.

When goods are received which have not been ordered, then refusal to accept and return is advisable in every case. Again, unsaleable stock results in heavy mark-downs.

Price changes between the time of order and delivery must be accepted, but notification by the supplier should be received in order to avert wrong prices on tickets and advertising.

Merchandise sent without confirmation orders should always be returned. Any gentleman's agreement should be avoided as these leave a buyer open to exploitation.

The return of merchandise to a supplier should be done through the agent or representative so that authority is first obtained. The observation of this code leads to the building of excellent business relationships between retailer and supplier.

When merchandise fails to meet the standard of the sample or the specifications of the Institute of British Standards, then return should be made.

The cancellation of orders should only be done before the original order has reached the supplier. Special orders should be put into stock and never cancelled if a customer changes her mind and refuses delivery.

The deduction of discount other than the rate agreed is unethical and authority to do this should be obtained first. This simple code serves to increase the goodwill between the supplier and the retailer who stands as the last link in the chain of production.

7.8 SYNDICATE PROBLEMS

BUYING TECHNIQUES

1. Define the difference between the principles and techniques of buying.

2. How is information assembled to estimate sales, purchases and stock levels?

3. How necessary is a buying plan?

4. Compare and contrast central buying and store buying, and the advantages and disadvantages.

5. How can classification be used as a buying technique?

6. What influences affect sales planning?

7. Construct a medium term plan for a basic range of merchandise, sales totalling £30,000 and stock totalling £70,000.

8. Discuss the advantages of grouping in order to buy on a large scale.

9. Discount is a reward for efficiency. Discuss.

10. Define the ethical considerations in buying and discuss their application to modern retailing.

8.0

Stock Control

8.1 STOCK CONTROL

This is the term given to describe *the study of the movement of items of merchandise from entering the Store to leaving the counter.* On the other hand, merchandise control, dealt with in Chapter 10 is the study of book stocks, or stock figures.

Physical stock control embraces the following store procedure:

(1) Receipt procedure
(2) Marking and ticketing
(3) Stockroom procedure
(4) Counters and display

8.2 RECEIPT PROCEDURE

All incoming goods must be checked and counted against the carriers delivery sheet. Delivery is made by many companies, including British Rail Goods, Passenger, and British Road Services plus private road hauliers. Each parcel or carton must be signed for as undamaged, or where opened, damaged, wet, as damaged, and this is the first check against theft or damage. Claims arising always begin at this point.

The next stage is the detailed check of items against the packing note, normally a duplicate of the invoice. The goods are checked against the invoice before payment can be made to the supplier. Having carried out a detailed check, security of stocks is always vitally important as the merchandise passes into the stockroom or on to the counter. The struggle against pilferage is constant and in many stores cages are often used into which unauthorized persons are never admitted. This is practical where space allows central marking areas to be used. However, space being at a premium, merchandise more often passes directly to the department to be marked. Merchandise cannot be sold until it reaches the selling area, so this fact must determine priorities. Three checks have to be made: (1) parcels on receipt, (2) items against invoice or packing note, (3) the correct styles, quantities, colours against the order.

The sooner the selling price is introduced, the sooner the selling process can begin. Receipt procedure in some chain stores is very much simplified because each item does not have to be marked. It goes directly to the counter, or understock, to find its ultimate place under a single counter ticket carrying size and price details. In department stores each item receives its individual price ticket, which is, in comparison, a more costly process.

8.3   We may now summarize the full operation. Firstly, the store order is made out, a copy is sent to the supplier, a copy may be sent to the receiving room, a copy goes to the merchandise office and a copy stays in the department. Next, the merchandise office checks that the amount spent is within the open-to-buy figure and they mail the suppliers copy. The invoice is received, either prior to delivery, or immediately afterwards. The merchandise is then received from the supplier and the items are checked in detail against the invoice. The selling

ORDER PROCEDURE

Store   Manufacturer

Receiving Room

Factory

Departmental Order

Office

Merchandise
Office

Order _____   Stock ,—.—— ..——.. —
Invoice ....   Payment ._ .——.——.

price is affixed and this price is marked on the invoice to be extended at selling on an extension invoice. Goods are placed in stock, or are displayed. The cost invoice and the selling invoice are sent to the merchandise office, where some stores prefer that the selling extensions are completed. When the selling total is recorded the invoice passes to the ledger office for payment, bearing its cost and selling prices.

Many variations on this scheme are operated in stores, but the same general principles are applied and variations occur mainly for reasons of size and the degree of automated equipment used. Accurate receipt and invoicing procedures are essential if good stocktaking results are to be attained at the end of each year. Accurate pricing is essential so that assistant and customer are left in no doubt that only one price exists.

8.4 MARKING AND TICKETING

Marking methods vary greatly. Chains have printed price cards, small stores may print a whole history in code on the label. Price lining offers the most economical method and cuts confusion or proliferation of individually priced items. The sole object of marking should be the identity of price in order to make a sale. Price tickets are silent salesmen. Used simply and effectively, they eliminate the haggling process and aid the elements of self-selection. Customers gain confidence only when they know that there is one price and everybody is happy to pay.

Price tickets were first introduced in the nineteenth century and Wannamaker of New York were the first to use them throughout their store. Pre-printed tickets used, for example by Marks and Spencer on their counters, are the cheapest and most effective method, limited to basic lines adaptable to self-selection only. Foods in packets or cans lend themselves to speedy stamping methods, but these would be eliminated by price lining. Expensive items are individually priced with swing tickets and the details may be a selection from the following:

Retail Price	Cost price in code
Delivery date in code	Stock group or section
Supplier in code	Season by letter or ticket colour
Invoice number	Tax in code

The main essential is the retail selling price. Other details are less important and may only be written in off-peak periods.

8.5 STOCKROOM PROCEDURE

The use of stockrooms in any store other than the very large ones is under attack due to staff and space costs and stockrooms are coming more under the supervision and operation of the sales department. The accumulation of obsolete stock is a critical problem of stockroom procedure and is difficult to prevent unless measures are taken to ensure efficient supervision. The regular stock count is one method and this reduces the accumulation of bad stock. Counts of stock vary according to the type of department.

The following count may be operated every fortnight for a basic stock range. First, list the lines and break each down in detail as required. Count the quantity and enter on the catalogue. On receipt of each packing note or invoice (the packing note is better), include the quantity received in the receipt column. Add the previous stock and the receipts and put this figure in the total column. When the stock is counted in the next period this figure, when deducted from the total of the previous period, will give a sale figure for this item for the period between the counts, e.g.

		A	B	C	D	E
		Stock	Receipt	Total	Sale	Stock
Vests Interlock	Small	88	24	112	33	79
	Medium	118	48	166	68	98
	Large	74	12	86	22	64

Count column A first and put in the receipts B as the stock arrives. At the end of the period add and insert C. On completion of column E, the new stock level the sales are calculated by deducting E from C.

The count may be carried across a stock sheet for several count-periods and a study of the unit stock and unit sales is vital information for the correct balancing of stock levels.

8.6 COUNTERS AND DISPLAY

The stock received should reach the counter as soon as is practical. Here the rate of sale should be calculated so that counter space is allocated on a basis of footage per sales. The unit stock control system described in 8.5 can be applied for this task. Certain counters are better than others owing to their position in relation to customer flow, and this fact should be considered. The degree of self-selection depends on the nature of the merchandise, but this can be affected by the method of display. Strict stock control will serve to promote as well as protect the merchandise and is a very important part of sales promotion.

8.7 SYNDICATE PROBLEMS

STOCK CONTROL

1. Discuss the difference between Stock Control and Merchandise Control.

2. Discuss the practical problems of keeping stock in areas which are bolted and barred. What physical problems occur and how can theft be minimized without resort to these methods?

3. How does receipt procedure differ as between Chain and Department stores?

4. Describe in full the ordering, receipt and marking procedure operated in your store and comment on the problems arising.

5. How much information is required on tickets and how should the allocation of time for this operation be planned?

6. Why is invoice procedure of prime importance to each department?

7. When customers ask for a reduction in the price of an item already marked, what procedure can the buyer adopt?

8. How necessary is a periodic stock count on (*a*) basic range, (*b*) a non-basic range?

9. Discuss the factors to be considered in compiling a fortnightly unit stock control system.

10. What information would a buyer expect to obtain from a full stock counting system operated monthly?

9.0

Stock-keeping

9.1 Having received and marked incoming stock, we must now turn our attention to the counter and display. The jungle, as it is commonly termed among retail staff, is the most important and vital part of the store. In the activity and movement of stock can lie the greatest source of stock shortage. The correct handling of goods is important to business and industry alike and special courses on handling goods are available for employees. Certain basic principles may be recognized.

9.2 Cleanliness is the first factor we must consider. All stock must look fresh, new and compelling to the customer. Whether it be food or textiles, methods of packaging to a standard of clinical cleanliness are constantly being sought. Polythene wraps are useful, but they fail to allow the customer to handle the merchandise, thus hindering complete product knowledge, which is seldom available at a glance. Unless these wrappers are treated chemically they attract dust. Colour is a very important factor, both in floor covering, lighting, décor and backgrounds of fixtures. The first daily duty of each assistant should be to dust and check stocks so that soiled items can be segregated immediately, ready for disposal.

9.3 The presentation of goods is very important. Here the main requirement is motivation, or promotion of ideas, both in display, but also in teaming items in pairs or sets. All stocks should be accessible to the customer. The design of fixtures constantly moves towards maximizing accessibility, which in turn encourages self-selection. This tends also to minimize the shortcomings of sales assistants when service and selling ability are at a premium. Eagerness to learn product use and application, eager and ready enthusiasm and ability to display, demonstrate and sell—all these qualities and trained skills are vital training areas. However, training the assistant to keep adequate forward reserves of stock and a correct sequence from stock-room selling fixture, is basic. Rules of procedure seem to depend more on the individual head of department rather than on simple store procedures prepared for all departments. An example of sizing immediately springs to mind. In all cases customers read from left to right, yet without supervision an assistant will rarely carry this through. Her sizes run to suit the fixture, or her personal preference. By keeping small sizes to the left and displaying each larger size to the right, she enables a customer to read the size range and encourages self-selection. 'Controlled housekeeping' may sum up the problem of training good assistants. Rotate stock on a first in, first out basis, run the sizing scale logically, group the merchandise, and control the display. The simple schemes of stock-keeping are most effective because they allow quick checks and accurate counts to be carried out at regular intervals. Control results in systematic counts, which in turn enable swift checks to be carried out, and this makes re-ordering simple and efficient. Sales are lost if this process is not efficiently operated. All sales promotion springs from this point of customer reaction. As the urge to buy is satisfied, the stock must be replenished, or, in the case of a single consignment, further promotions must be prepared to follow.

9.4 STOCK SHORTAGE

The aim of stock-keeping is to produce a balanced range, to prevent overstocking and to control stock shortage. Shortage may be divided:
(1) Calculation
(2) Causes

CALCULATION

The calculation of shortage begins with the physical stock-take. This produces a ledger stock, or an opening stock. All invoices passed for payment are added to this during the period, whilst all sales are deducted. This is normally a process carried out daily, with results weekly. At the end of a year these figures give a book total of stock that each department should hold. Debits and credits should be balanced and affect this total.

Customer and staff discounts are deducted. Mark-downs must be deducted. When the physical stocktake is completed in the department, the final figure is compared with the book figure and the difference is the departmental overage or shortage.

Opening stock	£10,000
Purchases	£90,000
	£100,000
Sales	£91,000
	£9,000

If the physical stock count result was £8,800, a shortage of £200 would result, or 2·2% shortage.

CAUSES

The central problem of shortage control, then, is the accuracy of ledger accounts on the one hand and the accuracy of stock-keeping, selling and stock counting on the other. Whilst the process of calculation is straightforward, the control of causes is infinitely more difficult. The main causes are two-fold:

(1) Clerical error
(2) Physical loss

Clerical Error
  (*a*) Clerical errors on ledgers.
  (*b*) Errors in carrying forward sales figures or stock figures in the merchandise office.
  (*c*) Failure to record mark-downs in the ledger.
  (*d*) Goods charged but not received.
  (*e*) Miscalculations of selling prices on invoices.

Physical loss
  We must subdivide physical loss and also attempt to simplify the causes under six main categories:

(*a*) *Theft*
  Theft may occur at any stage from initial receipt in the stock-room, to the counter. This then, is theft by staff. Also, through bad till procedure, cash thefts may occur. At the counter the customer may pilfer stock without payment, or staff may under-

sell goods to friends or relatives. Recent convictions for this type of crime have risen sharply and the problem of theft must be tackled by every assistant, supervisor or manager so that blind spots are eliminated and alertness to service minimizes the effects.

(b) Breakage

Any packaged item is liable to deteriorate if badly handled. Fragile goods must be marked so that special care in handling is ensured, but all stages of handling are important and training in this sphere of operations is essential. The utilization of stockroom area is essential.

(c) Loss

Losses in transit have steadily increased in the recent past and there are no signs that this trend can be reversed. Accurate checking on receipt for opened parcels and cartons is essential in order to make claim against the carriers. As self-service is applied to more departments, the temptation to steal increases and the saving in staff costs may be lost, partially, as theft by customers increases. Theft by staff can be minimized by vigilance, open-plan fixtures and organized facilities for staff purchasing. This should include an area for personal shopping bags, where all purchases can be checked. Till procedure must be controlled by the simple rule of cash first and pack goods later. This enables a check to be kept on the amount rung in the till and prevents the assistant from the temptation of pocketing the cash from a sale for which the customer has tendered the exact amount in cash and has not waited for a receipt.

(d) Physical Shrinkage

In food stock many commodities lose weight through evaporation. Weight loss affects the final quantity sold and can cause a loss of profit. Likewise, in fashion stocks the problem is soilage. Fitting the garment may cause this, dust falling on displayed stock, or unprotected stock may be the main contributory causes. Unless every mark-down is recorded a loss will occur.

(e) Mis-measuring

This occurs both in weighing the food ranges, or in measuring materials by the yard. Assistants should not be allowed to serve friends or relatives, for this provokes the extra piece and, over a period of time, produces a loss.

(f) Over-selling

This is again the problem of selling to a relative or friend when the price marked on the article is not charged. The difference is not recorded in the mark-down book and therefore produces a loss.

The great problem may be summed up as one of pin-pointing the probable area of loss. Lord Marks once stated that the only effective way to prevent theft in a store is to keep the doors closed and bolted. The most effective safeguards, therefore, are open plan fixtures and vigilance on the part of every member of the selling team. Where statistics show above average losses, then management must probe the causes, using methods of test purchasing and observations of this kind to detect and apprehend the culprits. Open plan layout provides maximum visibility and is an excellent safeguard. Positioning of tills is important as theft from tills by customer or staff must be made easy to detect. Self-service counters are given so much attention by shop lifters that glass protection has been evolved which protects against theft without weakening the impulse to select and purchase. The only real answer to theft problems is good supervision. There is no other complete solution.

As detection in a large store is difficult, owing to the great number of staff and customers involved, management may call upon the services of agencies who will send teams of trained shoppers to carry out test purchases. The checking of staff at the exit is a very important safeguard. All new staff should be trained to understand the theft problems during initial training.

RULES FOR THE PREVENTION OF PILFERING

THE DO'S

(1) Do be alert at all times.
(2) Do reduce temptation to steal by constant vigilance.

(3) Do watch displays of self-service type.

(4) Do ensure adequate lighting of stocks.

(5) Do supervise expensive merchandise constantly.

(6) Do supervise all staff purchases at exits.

(7) Do alert the staff at all peak periods.

(8) Do recognize known shop lifters.

(9) Do recognize the type of clothing worn by shop lifters and their methods.

(10) Do pay special attention to the lingering customer who repeatedly returns to one spot.

THE DON'TS

(1) Don't display below eye level.

(2) Don't accost and accuse unless certain.

(3) Don't accost without a manager or security staff.

(4) Don't use force with, or threaten suspects.

(5) Don't prevent suspect from leaving the premises.

(6) Don't approach until over the threshold.

(7) Don't be negative; act quickly and effectively.

If loss through shop lifting could be eliminated overnight estimates of around 2 per cent of total sales revenue would be saved. In other words, prices could be reduced by this amount if lifters were eliminated. This is a universal problem and is being met by larger fines and more publicity. The retailer can only combat loss by vigilance, the training of staff and the sensible organization of fixtures, fittings and position of tills.

9.5 SYNDICATE PROBLEMS

STOCK-KEEPING

1. How can a manager delegate to the supervisor the tasks of good housekeeping? Define the specific tasks.

2. Assistants who display well, are they born or trained to these important tasks?

3. What is meant by 'good presentation of stock' and what can be done to raise the standard if it leaves no impression?

4. What are the main causes of clerical shortages of stock?

5. Examine the main causes of stock shortage.

6. Are store rules and regulations sufficient to prevent stock

shortage or should the prevention of pilferage depend on sound supervision?

7. As a departmental manager, would you support the store detective or depend on the word of a senior sales assistant?

10.0

Merchandise Control

10.1 PLANNING STOCK LEVELS

In Chapter 7 we discussed the techniques a buyer must use in order to interpret the open to buy position. This consists of the computation of sets of figures of sales stock and purchases. We have seen that the aim of merchandising is to increase stockturn by controlling the stock level and by increasing sales. As retailing departments have become more complicated, so the need for simple classification has developed. We must now see the difference between stock control and merchandise control. Stock control we have seen is physical in terms of how stock items are kept in order to promote sales and prevent loss. Merchandise control, on the other hand, is *the calculation of stock value in order to prevent overstock, low stockturn, or loss of sales through under-stock*. This ensures an optimum use of the space allocated to each department and gives information to management as regards the performance of each department.

10.2 In chain store management the main pre-occupation of all levels of store staff is sales promotion. In departmental store management the effort is widely deployed in buying and in sales promotion. This element is crucial for department stores. Is effort too widespread? Should concentration be centred on administration by office staff and on sales promotion by the sales staff. Too often these two functions are confused so that the operation malfunctions owing to lack of concentration on selling and promotion.

10.3 We must now consider the problems presented to a buyer on receipt of the planned figures and the actual sales, commitment and stock, and examine the various ways performance can bend the actual result to meet the planned figures.

First, the plan is only a plan and circumstances alter cases, but real effort must be exerted at all times to achieve the planned figures. Two problems emerge, low sales and high stocks. Each are interdependent, for when planned sales are not achieved, planned stocks become too high, so that purchases must be cut. Purchases must be reduced wisely, so that basic stocks are kept in, whilst non-basics are reduced. Thus the seasonal, or high risk stock should take the main cut. Customers never forgive a store which fails to satisfy basic needs, but will bear with a store if selection is limited in the short run.

Planned stock levels must be interpreted flexibly by the buyer. An adequate assortment of basics must be provided at all times and merchandise control must be aimed at directing stock figures towards this end.

10.4   In a period of expansion when national productivity rises, buying tends to be less rigidly controlled and this freedom from restraints does boost the increased selling period. The process of deceleration acts conversely in time of austerity or 'freeze'. A lost sale is then not as important as a large overstock. In a period of recession or contraction, when national productivity tends to fall, the extra care exercised in purchasing reduces sales. Price falls expected in this situation rarely pass down to the retailer and analysis of recent trade fluctuations shows a steady rise.

The traditional periods of increased activity, Easter, Whitsun, Summer Bankholiday, have lost part of their stimulus, and customers are buying items of wardrobe replacement today, rather than buying in quantity because the season has changed. Weather over the past decade has influenced this, but the higher standard of living, the increase in heating systems, and affluence, are the main factors in the changing habits of buying public.

10.5   A further factor to consider is the changing pattern of accounting systems. Large groups, such as Debenhams, are able to enter the computer age ahead of the many smaller groups and stores. Management decisions can be based on information gathered today from many diverse sources, rather than from last week or even last month.

We have seen how the main stock build-up is made immediately before peak demand. As the peaks alter according to the factors just considered, the need for immediate merchandising information on the sales floor is pressing. To get the right assortment at the right time requires interpretation of the sterling figure to units of stock as early as possible. A buyer must become adept at breaking down bulk sterling into stock ratios and classification and must constantly think in terms of ratios of sizes, colours, types, styles so that purchases can be balanced.

10.6 STOCK PLANNING

There are four simple methods of stock planning in use:
(1) Basic stock planning.
(2) Percentage variation method.
(3) Week's supply method.
(4) Stock-Sales-ratio method.

BASIC STOCK PLANNING

The first requirement is to calculate the minimum stock in each category of each item. This is catalogued and regularly counted. Each line is listed separately so that it can be studied in detail, in sizes or colours, for example. A more sophisticated development of this system would require the receipts to be entered and these added to the stock levels would give sales per item. A study of the amount of stock required to keep in stock at each peak and quiet period reveals the various basic levels for each period:

10.6A *Cardigans Style X*	*Size*	*Basic low*	*Basic high*
Retail selling price	32″	2	4
average 30/-	34″	4	6
	36″	6	10
	38″	4	6
	40″	2	3

Thus eighteen are needed in the off-peak, and twenty-nine in the peak and stocks of this style should be kept at these levels. Having extended the study to all lines which must be considered basic merchandise, i.e. lines which sell for the major part of each season and vary little in price, a total figure for

10.6B   STERLING TRANSLATED TO STOCK

£10,000 sterling total value of stock		1st Buyer translates	2nd Buyer translates	3rd Buyer translates
	Dining Suites	30%	20%	25%
	Bedroom Suites	30%	45%	15%
				35%
	Lounge Suites	25%	15%	
	Miscellaneous	15%	20%	25%

all basic stock within each section can be calculated.

The basic stock is calculated by adding the sales to the difference between the average stock and the average sales.

e.g. *Stock required=Sales for period+(average stock for season—average monthly sales)*

10.6C

If the sales for March were £10,000
If the sales for April were £13,000
Stockturn planned 4·0
The six-monthly sales=£60,000
The average monthly stock$=\dfrac{£60,000}{4}=£15,000$

Stock required March 1 = 10,000 + (15,000 — 10,000) = 15,000
Stock required April 1 = 13,000 + (15,000 — 10,000) = 18,000

Thus a basic stock can be maintained and a high rate of stockturn is made, plus a seasonal range on which a lower stockturn is made. Further consideration may lead to the stock being increased at the beginning of a peak month, i.e. before the peak selling period. Also provision may be made in purchasing for constant replenishment of basic merchandise. The only problem arises when, at the beginning of the half-year, overstock is carried from the previous half-year. Allowance must therefore be made for this contingency. Finally, seasonal trends must be provided for so that full advantage can be taken of risk and seasonal selling.

PERCENTAGE VARIATION METHOD

The percentage fluctuation in monthly stocks should be half as great as the percentage fluctuations in monthly sales as compared with average sales. e.g. When monthly sales are 20 per cent above average monthly sales, the stocks should be increased by half this, or 10 per cent.

EXAMPLE 10.6D January sales=£150
Average monthly sales=£120
Increase is $\dfrac{30}{120}=25\%$ on av. monthly sales
Average monthly stocks=£200
January stocks=$200+12\frac{1}{2}\%=£225$

This method tends to be academic, and is not widely used in Britain, and in any case should be applied only to sections with a high stockturn. A rate of 6·0 per year may be taken as a minimum viable level at which this formula may be applied. For stores with a half-yearly merchandise control cycle, this is not a feasible method. The variation method should be confined to those sections which need a month-by-month guide figure and are confined solely to fast basics.

WEEK'S SUPPLY METHOD

This is a method generally used as a guide to chain store merchandising. As we have seen, the main object of management at store level is to promote sales. The complicating factors of stockturn, pricing, special orders, do not apply and the lines are selected by a separate team. This simplified technique is therefore easily guided by this simple calculation.

First calculate the sales of each line per week. Then calculate the upward or downward trend of sales. Calculate the mimimum stock required to promote the line, add to this the stock to offset the delivery period from the time of the order date, to the delivery date.

EXAMPLE 10.6E

Week	1	2	3	5	6	7	8	9
Sales £'s	50	55	60	61	59	62	55	40

In theory, the sales of week 1, £50, require only week 2 and week 3 stock, i.e. £115. If this were the case, in practice we would be completely out of stock within 14 days. If we had deliveries within the next week of £55 and £60 the following week, then sales could be maintained on the minimum stock. This brings the problem of delivery into focus. If supplies were always available, stocks could be drastically cut. The delay in the time from ordering to delivery accounts for high stock. Thus the period before peak demand would require 6-8 weeks stock with two weeks stock on order and in the pipe line and a further two weeks supply about to be sent off to the store. Thus instead of holding the minimum of £115, we would need a minimum of £285 in stock in order to prevent running out of stock. If we apply this rule of thumb method to our stockturn theory, given a stockturn of 8·0 this would correspond with

$$\frac{52 \text{ weeks}}{8} = 6\tfrac{1}{2} \text{ weeks stock.}$$

Therefore $6\tfrac{1}{2}$ weeks sales figures gives the stock requirement. The method of control is thus suited to fast basics and changes in relation to the selling season. Delivery is the unknown factor, but the method is simple and taking an average of eight weeks stock would tend to shock departmental controllers by the number of departments that are over this stock figure.

STOCKS-SALES RATIO

Research into the relations of stocks and sales reveals a direct relationship between the two. It has been established that the ratio is 2. This means that if sales are £100, stock of £200, or a ratio of 1 : 2.

This simple system would be useless for sections where the sales fluctuate considerably within a short period of time. It serves, however, as quick check method.

10.7 All the above methods are mathematical formulae designed to calculate the optimum stock level for various types of merchandise, giving a stock level of variable proportion geared to the expected rate of sale. Fluctuations in sales which are not included in last year's figures tend to upset stock calculations. New lines, so essential to the store image, defeat accurate assessment, but buying power must be reserved for these.

10.8 SYNDICATE PROBLEMS

MERCHANDISE CONTROL

1. What do we mean by merchandise control?

2. How can the department store buyer divide time between sales promotion and buying and plan each phase of the operation successfully?

3. In achieving and in planning there may exist a problem of poor sales or over-buying, or both. How can these two factors be reconciled?

4. Why is the stock plan vital to each department? What method of planning would be adopted for a basic range?

5. Should stock be planned on the basis of the level of the same period last year, or on the level required for the next period last year?

6. If the stock level of a department is too high, how can the level be reduced without lowering the sales figure? Should this be a short term or a long term problem?

7. Merchandise control depends on sterling figures. How best can these be translated into units of stock?

8. The objective of control is to produce an expected pattern or to relieve spending power to promote more risk merchandise. What factors should be considered here?

9. What is understood by the term 'commitment control' and what part do commitment figures play in planning?

10. Describe the relations between 'sales', 'purchases' and 'stocks'.

11.0

Causes and Control of Slow Moving Stock

11.1   The wide range and assortment of merchandise required in a department store will in all cases produce some slow lines. The problem here is one of control. From our study of model stock plans it may be seen that the fringe sizes tend to sell more slowly than the main sizes. In the same way, some colours are slower and certain styles are difficult to sell. As all systems of stock control should be evolved in order to adjust levels, the underlying aim must be to increase the volume of fast sellers and curb the buying of slow merchandise. When stocks are analysed and when specialization results from this process, then sales will increase. By rigidly controlling slow stock, the main investment is made in fast stock and this increases the stockturn rate. As a reputation for the ability to supply anything from stock has become the policy of some departmental stores, and this is seen by many customers to be the general image of this type of store, this infinite range imposes a heavy price, except, for example in central London, where the most diversified population may be found. The examples of successful businesses run on these principles tend to be fewer outside densely populated areas. A high rate of turnover is essential to the adjustment of stocks and the increase of stockturn.

11.2   By definition, slow merchandise must be *all lines which turn less times than the planned stockturn rate.* This includes not only the slow sellers, but also those lines held in such depth that whilst sales are high, they fall below the stockturn rate for the department as a whole. This would also include out-of-season lines which normally sell fast. The stock level must therefore be phased out sooner to prevent stock being left on the shelves. This group would consist mainly of lines kept for special customers and specialist merchandise. As we

have seen, if the stockturn rate is planned at 6·0, then the average life of stock in that section should be $52 = 8\frac{2}{3}$ i.e $8\frac{2}{3}$
$$\overline{6}$$
weeks in stock. The buyer should regard all stock over nine weeks old as slow selling merchandise, and in this context delivery of stock must be in small quantities that are received frequently.

An alternative method which will give a quantitative analysis of slow stock is the comprehensive system of unit stock control. The calculation of stock and sales of each line enables a balance to be kept both in quantity, delivery timing and in the number of transactions per line during each period. Any line which sells at a slower rate than the planned stockturn rate can be seen at a glance. This, then, has become a standard procedure in most group stores, especially for central buying organizations where information is required quickly, to be collected and processed for the whole organization.

One final method must be noted, where the calculation of slow stock depends on the comparison of the rate of sales with the average stocks. This is normally computed as an annual rate and is then compared with the planned stockturn rate.

11.3 The main causes of slow-moving stock may be traced to the motivation of the sales assistant. It is a human tendency to enthuse more about the new than the old. If old stock were to be shown first in every case and sold, as the first in, first out principle would suggest, then less old stock would accumulate. It is harder to create enthusiasm for old lines, systems of ticketing or coded systems of datal history are ineffective when the assistant meets the customer. A complete knowledge of stocks and motivation by supervisor or management is essential and there is no substitute for this. Where a coloured ticket is used to indicate the birthday of the stock, this is an aid to control. Control depends on methodical stock checks so that attention can be focussed on lines which must be given special promotion in order to eliminate them.

11.4 A detailed system of stock control should reveal the stock composition in detail so that re-ordering may be done accurately. If this is not done, continued investment in slow lines aggravates the stock position and slows down the stock-turn rate. Where seasonal stock must be eliminated early to prevent slow sellers from appearing towards the end of a season, the bulk of the intake must be taken early, the end of the season being used for repeats, filling in gaps in the range and for special orders. Some stores use systems of special incentives to sell old stock, the so-called 'spivs'. Yet incentives of this kind may work towards the deliberate creation of old stock by the assistant, in order to earn the higher rate of commission.

11.5   Control by unit stock control systems must produce the problem of disposal of old stock. Early buying should reduce this problem as must the hiving off of basic ranges in fast moving, continuity lines. Yet the exact conditions, the timing and precision needed to prevent slow sellers, rarely combine in exactly the required way. Mark-downs become necessary at a late stage in the season, often dictated in timing by the date of the half-yearly Sale event. The clearing of seasonal stock is vital to the success of the next season. Two methods of clearing are possible, firstly mark-down, and secondly sales promotion. The method of mark-down should be retained as a last resort, since this is negative as far as profitability is concerned. Sales promotion as a method is positive and entails prominent display during the peak selling times plus advertising where necessary. This gives impetus to the effort of selling.

11.6   A further method of eliminating slow stock is to group and sell in larger than normal quantities, e.g. three cakes for 1/-. This will sell more cakes than a ticket announcing 5d. per cake. This method of combination selling also lends itself well to grouping plus a mark-down. In durables it is sometimes possible to get the supplier to take back certain items for a limited period and then take a re-delivery when the line is demanded. In groups, slow stock may be returned to the central warehouse, or transferred to branches where the season continues for a longer period.

11.7   No method of elimination is equal to the buyer who by sound stock control merchandises only the stock that will sell.

Service is the vital part of selling and sources of quick replacement must be lined to quick turnover. Foods are the best example. Sampling pilot quantities to gain more precise statistics before large orders are placed helps to eliminate slow sellers. With local suppliers, their strengths and weaknesses can easily be assessed and strengths can play an important part in the scheme. Finally, rigid control of special orders is needed, for if these are not claimed they may prove to be very slow lines.

Concentration on part of one's field or trade leads a store towards a simple image, which customers are very quick to appreciate. The faster the movement of stock within a department, the more the customer is encouraged to look critically and analytically at the ranges offered. The more she knows and understands of a firm's policy and capability, the more she is likely to be loyal in her spending habits.

11.8 SYNDICATE PROBLEMS

CAUSES AND CONTROL OF SLOW MOVING STOCKS

1. How can a buyer calculate a ratio of sizes in order to ensure that slow stocks are reduced to a minimum?
2. Define the term 'slow moving stock'. How can this be detected and prevented?
3. If two assistants on a department produce high levels of slow stock (Miss X) and very few slow lines (Miss Y), what action can the buyer take?
4. What factors determine the choice between eliminating slow stock by mark-down or by a special sales promotion?
5. What steps can be taken to eliminate the slow line?
6. On taking over a run-down department, which would take precedence, the causes of the poor stock, or a sound system of stock control?

12.0
Sales Promotion

12.1   Sales promotion is *communication between retailer and consumer by using the facilities in the store to achieve planned sales targets.*

Sales promotion in stores is a combination of these main factors:
1. Display—windows, internal sales areas.
2. Advertising—branding—packaging.
3. Staff motivation, training.
4. Demonstration.
5. Special events.
6. Creative merchandising.

12.2   DISPLAY

Display is one method of communicating the broad image of the business by translating the policy of the Board in visual terms. The customer easily interprets a high-, medium- or low-class image. Display management has three main areas of operation:

(*a*) Windows.

(*b*) Internal display.

(*c*) Display preparation room.

WINDOWS

Windows should attract and motivate customers to enter the store. Where a store communicates an image well, e.g. Marks and Spencer Ltd., Woolworth, Harrods, for example, the latter relies very much on the creative image, the others less so and Marks and Spencer have almost reduced windows to a few groups of merchandise separating street and store. Windows should carry certain messages:

1. *Sales volume.* Store policy and image is promoted in window display. A need must be stimulated, causing a decision to enter the store. Sales volume is the result and in part the

display management and staff carry this responsibility.

2. *New customers.* Windows must stimulate both new customers to enter as well as established clientele. The message must be vital, simple and understandable to achieve this.

3. *Stimulation.* Window space should be allocated on a basis of planned sales development. Windows should not 'belong' to departments. The allocation should be based on policy of quality, image factor, novelty, exclusivity or branding. Where allocation is done on a basis of turnover, the growth potential of smaller departments may never be realized. As a form of communication, the window allocation may warrant a new basis of allocation providing for novelty and innovation.

4. *Acceleration of slow stock.* Old stock should never be promoted in windows except during clearance sales or special events of this type. Clearly, when stock has reached the end of its average life in terms of stockturn, then window display may prevent high mark-down in the future.

5. *Classification.* Windows promote groups of merchandise and help to educate the public to accept the grouping of stock within the store. This should help customers to locate stocks.

6. *Cleanliness.* Window stock must at all times be immaculately clean and well pressed when possible. This reflects the general standards of the store. Any deviation creates a bad impression.

7. *Seasonal display.* The stock in windows should precede the peak selling periods. This communicates a forward looking image, but more important, it creates needs in the near future. The customer is then able to prepare to purchase.

8. *Ticketing.* Where style and quality is paramount, then ticketing is less important as the factor of price is not important to this type of customer. Where price is important to the customer, this should be shown in the window. Information on tickets should be carried on tickets with a ticket design uniformly selected to reflect the image factor.

9. *New lines.* The window is the best medium for communication and demonstration of new merchandise. Sight of the product stimulates. Any previous advertising or editorial comment will aid decision making at this stage.

INTERNAL DISPLAY

Internal display work is often left to juniors or inexperienced staff. Eye movement tests in supermarkets and consumer tests show that 50 per cent of the decisions to purchase are made inside supermarkets. This emphasizes the importance of impulse buying and the need for a professional approach to all internal display work. Professional standards depend on the training ability of display management.

DISPLAY PREPARATION ROOM

The need for a professional approach to training cannot be neglected and equipment in the form of a dummy window and space to prefabricate the props for all types of display requires space.

12.3 ADVERTISING—BRANDING—PACKAGING

These three inter-related factors are important in sales promotion. Advertising must be co-ordinated with national campaigns, stock levels and display. Many promotions fail because one or more of these factors are neglected. The advertising manager must decide how much is to be spent, media to be used, frequency of insertion, the size of the advertisement and co-ordinate the advertising with buying and display.

Branding is essentially an identification mark, or name, adopted to build an image and create repeat sales through brand loyalty. This gives management a unique brand which cannot be priced down by competitors and alternatively, can be used as a loss leader or a high profit earner. Tesco recently changed their brand name to 'Tesco' and doubled sales on each line through better identification. Marks and Spencer Ltd. have built up a quality image by up-grading merchandise, by the constant use of the 'St. Michael' brand, by laboratory tests and quality control. A brand can give flexibility in competitive price situations where R.P.M. has been replaced by suggested selling prices. Advertising a house brand is simple communication and can be linked with the store name or quality image, or with a keen pricing policy.

Packaging is a sales promotion technique and many tests on colour and message have been carried out. Size of pack, transportation, handling qualities, usage and description are essential factors.

12.4 STAFF MOTIVATION

All sales promotion depends on people. Training is essential to prepare staff for a sales promotion, but in the long run their energy, drive, enthusiasm, knowledge and professionalism will achieve results. Training of all grades of staff, sales and services, supervisors and management is essential if the policy of the Board is to be effective.

12.5 DEMONSTRATION

A professional demonstrator is a first class communicator. This form of sales promotion has links with history and the packman. His vital interest is gathering a crowd and using the maximum number of senses, sight, hearing, possibly taste or smell to sell his wares. His nature is extrovert and he may provide an excellent model for training sales staff if camera and tape recorder are used to capture the sequence and action. Many of our sales staff who are timid or shy might benefit. A demonstration adds interest to a store. It is highly personal selling.

12.6 SPECIAL EVENTS

Among the best promotions, from a turnover angle, we must consider the January and Mid-Summer Sales. On these two occasions all departments operate together with a single theme. The Sales period depends for success on psychological impulse based on low price. Behaviour is irrational, especially on the first morning. Other special events, e.g. Birthday Sales, Gift Weeks, Holiday Weeks, are special promotions of normal branded lines using the normal channels of sales promotion, windows, internal display, ticketing and packaging.

12.7 CREATIVE MERCHANDISING

Ideas for new products or the development of existing products originate from customer enquiries or comments. However these ideas seldom reach the manufacturers. The drive for creation and development comes, in the main, from manufacturers. Yet, well trained staff can pass ideas to buyers, who in turn could pass them on to respective suppliers. Consumer Associations may help in this respect and customers are using these services more, as encouragement is given to voice constructive criticism or active communication. This requires to be analysed, not only by interested manufacturers, but by the retail trade as well. The need for market research tools in the retail trades is vital to progress. Primary research on internal records, we have seen, has definite benefits. Survey work, panels and consumer tests are not yet used to examine reaction. The close contact between retail staff and customer is no defence against this criticism. Subjective analysis needs replacing by objective testing and it is in this direction that staff must be trained in the future. After-sales service may also reveal basic defects in product design and may lead to product improvement. Again the systematic use of communication is the basic problem.

12.8   SYNDICATE PROBLEMS

SALES PROMOTION

1. What is understood by the term 'sales promotion'?

2. How can the principles of sales promotion be used to balance stock levels?

3. Should the buyer motivate the display staff with the theme of the stock to be displayed, or should the display staff use stock to elaborate a theme?

4. What factors should be considered in planning a sales promotion?

5. Why does a composite promotion produce higher sales than a single effort?

6. What is 'creative merchandising'?

7. What part does motivation play in a successful sales promotion?

8. What are the aims of a professional display team?

9. A buyer has a problem of a slow line and decides to promote this by internal and window displays. At the same moment an invoice arrives for some fast, short supply, fashion lines. What factors determine his choice of promotional material?

10. Should display reflect to store image, or should it attract additional trade?

13.0

Salesmanship and Merchandising

13.1 THE NATURE OF THE SELLING PROCESS

Every person who enters the store is a potential customer. The motivating processes which create a desire to buy may be divided into three:

1. *Spending Power*

Social problems are not as important as income problems. The desire to buy must be supported by the ability to afford or the means of making the purchase.

2. *Emotion*

Instinct and emotion urge customers to examine their needs in relation to fear, hunger, the herd and the social scale.

3. *Reason*

Reason adds to the emotive forces and human nature allows thought and reason to project the desire for item B and C, dependent on the possession of item A.

Following the basic desire on the part of a potential customer, each individual sale follows a sequence of events, a pattern which is fairly consistent in all forms of selling. Most sales assistants are trained to follow this sequence and customers would find it strange if it were to be radically changed. Since each customer is individual in approach and needs, the assistant should treat each approach differently, but the sequence of procedure remains the same.

13.2 The process follows this pattern:

1. *Opening the sale*

At this first stage, welcome and study the customer. Find out the customer's needs by extracting information. From this, select the merchandise.

2. *Present the merchandise*

Select and demonstrate several items, allow handling, make known the selling points and discuss the quality and functions. Narrow the selection to two items.

3. *Handle the objections*

In narrowing the selection, the real needs are made known and the resistance can be met. Re-emphasize the appropriate selling points. Eliminate the objections by keeping the sale alive.

4. *Completing the sale*

Narrow the selection. Get a decision. Avoid a straight negative. If decision-making fails, return to a selling point and revive the objection state.

5. *Record the sale*

Rule of one customer, one bill, with every item on the bill.

6. *Closing the sale*

Assure the customer that the decision was wise, timed now, and the value was right. Thank the customer, build up good-will, final courtesies.

7. *Suggestion selling*

Introduce allied lines in any department.

The above stages may be alternated, permutated or changed, since each customer is different and this requires the exercising of flexibility. Failure to sell may occur at any of these stages, but where the assistant fails at one particular stage in a succession of sale interviews, this enables a trainer to improve on the weakness. Tuning in to a customer's wavelength comes naturally to some, but must be acquired by hard training in others. A pleasant personality plus a desire to give good service are the two main factors in choosing an assistant. Where self-selection has been introduced, stage 1 and 2 are effected by the customer. Staff, like customers, are individuals and react in many ways, but a constant factor that cannot change is well presented merchandise, well ticketed. The nub of the service problem seems, then, to depend on the use of self-service with intelligent assistants serving in an advisory capacity. This achieves the best result on a basis of turnover in relation to staff costs. In the final analysis, making a sale depends on the right merchandise and the customer's attitude of mind during the time spent in a department.

The most successful assistants possess unquenchable enthusiasm, bearing, a pleasant tone of voice, whilst mannerisms take second place. This enthusiasm in its very spontaneity seems to affect the customer and the interests of assistant and customer blend for a few moments. This seems to be the heart of service.

13.3 PERSONAL SALESMANSHIP
This is a highly individual characteristic, but we can categorize the main features:

1. *To be of good service to the customer*
This requires effort and creates goodwill. The word 'service' is one of the most overworked and least understood in stores of all types. To know and understand oneself and treat customers accordingly might define a concept near to an ideal.

2. *Accurate and comprehensive knowledge of merchandise*
However well suited to selling a personality may be, modern processes are becoming highly technical and a knowledge of the product, its composition and application is essential. The knowledge imparted becomes a technical service to the customer.

3. *Know your customer*
Store life mainly revolves around the problem of calculating and assessing other human beings and is in fact a human science. A retailer can better understand this problem by study of the various social areas in the British Isles. Personal characteristics vary from area to area, so that local knowledge is of great value.

Slow speech rarely equates the characteristics of slow wits and excessive help in making the final choice may result in a rebuffal and a lost sale. Often the nervous, impulsive type requires instant service and makes speedy decisions, so that the assistant must be prepared to catch up, in order to complete the sale. Silent customers need to be questioned to bring them into the selling process. This elicits an answering opinion. In this case a closed 'yes', or 'no', must be avoided by using open ended questions. The talkative customer must be steered by skilful demonstration. Only interrupt to make selling points and complete the sale. The argumentative customer must always evoke effort in order to retain goodwill. As Arnold Bennett said, 'The deliberate cultivation of the gift of putting yourself in the other person's place is the beginning of wisdom in human relations and the foundation of permanent good humour.' A very apt thought for our industry.

The qualities required in the sales assistant are numerous, but the responsibility of managers is to train and to train constantly. Thus, most persons can be developed and the traits to be cultivated are pleasantness, accuracy and enthusiasm for the merchandise. Development depends on four basic factors:

Physical
Health. Breath. Posture. Speech. Appearance. Dress.

Mental
Accuracy. Alertness. Imagination. Initiative. Job knowledge. Observation. Memory.

Social
Co-operation. Tolerance. Sympathy. Appreciation. Courtesy. Refinement.

Character
Truthfulness. Loyalty. Responsibility. Industriousness.

Briefly then, the ideal assistant is a person blended of these factors.

The practice of personal salesmanship may be defined as: The total selling effort within a store by the staff whose responsibility it is to serve customers and to promote the sale of goods that the store has to offer.

Easily definable needs result in simple sales. An undefinable need requires a technique of selection from a thousand items, only the selling process, personality and knowledge make a sale and enthusiasm helps this sequence along.

Self-service and self-selection are the processes of impersonal salesmanship. The first self-service store appeared in 1919, founded by the gay cavalier Clarance Saunders of Memphis, U.S.A. He began the Piggly Wiggly chain of stores subject to stock market manipulation in 1923, and Saunder's bankruptcy. A new concept of trading was born, however, and the traditional counter service, which had changed little since the Middle Ages now transferred the tasks of serving customers to the customers themselves and the sales assistant became a stock assistant. The rising costs of selling were to be contained and the cult of self-service has spread to banking, interior decorating and most branches of all service industries. Certain principles apply.

1. The customer must be able to select easily.
2. Must recognize various classifications and be able to collect the items.
3. Must carry the goods to a service point.

The more complicated an item of merchandise in design or function, the more personal salesmanship is required. Thus the simpler the item, the more readily it lends itself to self-service. Foods, haberdashery, hosiery, hardware, lines are well suited to this form of selling. Choice is left to the customer and the process of making a choice is self-selection. The process of collecting merchandise and carrying the items to service point is self-service. Careful use of these technical terms will avoid ambiguity. Self-selection has always been a strong factor in the selling process. Self-service is the technique developed from 1919, applied mainly to foods. The high wage costs and the competitive element which has tended to lower the profit margin together have speeded the development of self-service. Food items are bought very regularly and choice is made easy. Sections of canned goods, preserves, dairy produce, etc., easily classify, but meats and cheeses are more complex and personal service is given to discriminate between cuts and qualities. Once this simple and complex nature of merchandise is understood, rapid development may be expected in self-service.

Self-selection from catalogues, magazines and newspaper advertisements has developed rapidly. Small quantities only are initially merchandised until the reaction is tested and calculated so that bulk orders need only be considered after the customer has paid.

13.4   SYNDICATE PROBLEMS

SALESMANSHIP AND MERCHANDISING

1. Describe the nature of the selling process.
2. What are the differences between self-selection and self-service?
3. Define personal salesmanship. Are 'after sales service' and 'follow-up' factors of sales promotion?
4. How are staff costs calculated and how can the costs be contained or reduced?
5. What characteristics in the sales assistant make for success in selling? Can these be improved by training and what methods may be adopted? Is this a supervisor's responsibility or that of the buyer?
6. If the assistants employed are poor sellers, what methods may be adopted as regards merchandising and promotion?
7. Service is the most important factor in any store, what do we understand the word to mean?
8. Define the term self-service. To what categories of merchandise has it been applied and why?
9. If high wage costs are found to be a problem, should self-service principles be applied, or should the assistants be given intensive training, or should the assortment and selection of merchandise be examined critically?
10. Merchandise may only be bought for the assistant who can sell. Examine this statement and substitute a more dynamic policy of merchandising.

14.0

Conclusion

In the first place, the need to plan and to drill a store team so that plans are achieved, would seem to be the first priority. The need to train even the youngest member of the selling team in each department to understand the techniques employed is very long overdue. The effectiveness of any manager or buyer must depend on the degree of competence of those staff within his employ.

The dominance of sterling figures in stores has dominated the need to plan unit stocks. As a result, the keeping of unit stock cards has not been encouraged and merely forgotten and management are puzzled by the lack of knowledge regarding stock levels and quantities of goods sold. This responsibility belongs to buyer and middle management alone and is not carried through in all cases effectively.

Merchandising is the most fascinating art and should be a shared responsibility in all departments. When kept as a dark and lonely secret, the motivation of staff on receiving the latest or the most advanced design can be lost and retailing then loses the quality of novelty and surprise.

Basic stocks kept well, release the capital required to produce the changes and new trends and are a means to this end. Fashion or non-basic stocks impell new urges and produce the thrill of ownership which in our ultra-modern world, seems more elusive with every new season.

Bibliography

WINGATE & SCHALLER (1957) *Techniques of Retail Merchandising.* Prentice-Hall, 2nd ed.

CANFIELD, BERTRAND R. (1958) *Salesmanship Practices and Problems.* McGraw-Hill, 3rd ed.

DELENS, A. H. R. (1950) *Principles or Market Research* Crosby Lockwood.

HERZBERG & NICHOLSON (1952) *Training for Retail Sales Staff.* Pitman.

PASDERMADJIAN, H. (1954) *The Department Store.* Newman Books.

McLARNEY (1956) *Management Training Cases & Principles.* Richard D. Irwin Inc., 2nd ed.

SMALLBONE (1965) *The Practice of Marketing.* Staples Press, 3rd impression.

STACEY & WILSON (1958) *The Changing Pattern of Distribution.* Business Publications Ltd.

Index

Administration, 27
    control of, 28
    co-ordination of, 27
    direction of, 27
    organization of, 27
    planning of, 27
Advertising, 66

Bennett, Arnold, 72
Branding, 66
Buyer, 27
Buying,
    ethics of, 38–39
    fashion, 13
    habits, change of, 54
    Head Office, by, 34
    impulse, by, 7, 66
    overbuying, 11
    principles of, 27–32
    techniques of, 33–39
Buying Plan, 28, 33–39

Chain Stores, 3, 34
Class, trade of, see Trade
Cleanliness, store in, 65
Clerical Error, 48
Competition, 10, 16
Commission, 62
Communication, 27, 64, 68
Costs, staff, 29–30
Cost Price, 9, 13
Counters, display, 44
Customer,
    flow of, 4
    new, 64–65
    relations, 30

Department,
    management of, 29
    store of, 34
Discount, rates of, 38
Discounts, trade, 38
Display, 20, 44, 64–66
    seasonal, 64–65

Expenses, 14, 24

Goodwill, 23, 30–31
Gross Profit, see Profit

Lines,
    basic, 37, 54
    new, 65
    special, 16
Loss Leader, 15–16

Management,
    departmental, 29
    functions of, 2–3
Mark-down, 11, 24
Mark-up, 10, 13–16
Marshall, Alfred, 31
Merchandising,
    control, 53–58
    function, 1–8
    objectives, 5
    own-brand, 10, 66
    policy, 6

Open-To-Buy, 25

79

Packaging, 66
Price.
  fixing, 10
  lining, 18–20, 43
  planning, 9–12, 18–20
  reductions, 9–11, 19
Profit, 9–12
  gross, 13–15

Qualitative Analysis, 24
Quality, control, 2, 34
Quantity,
  control, 5
  discounts, 38

Receipt, procedure for, 41–43
R.P.M., Resale Price Mainten-
  ance, 21
Research, need for, 7
Residual Stock, 11
Retail Distributors Association,
  22
Retailing Policy, 2

Sales, 24–25
  forecasting, 33
  low, 54
  procedure, 69–71
  promotion, 64–68
  volume, 64
Salesmanship, 71–72
Sales Promotion, 30, 64–68
  advertising, 66

demonstrations, 67
display, 64
special events, 67
staff motivation, 67
Selection, 28
Self Selection, 7, 73
Self Service, 73
Selling Price, 9
  fixed, 13
Smith, Adam, 1
Staff, costs, 29–30
Stocks, high, 53–55
Stock,
  marking of, 43
  plan, basic, 35–37, 55–58
  residual, 11
  shortage of, 47–51
  shortage, physical of, 48–49
  slow, 60–63
Stockkeeping, 46–47
Stockroom, procedure, 44
Stockturn, rate of, 22–26
Supervision, 29, 50

Theft, 48
Ticketing, 43, 65
Timing, importance of, 2, 13, 35

Unit,
  shop, 1–3
  stock control, 62

Windows, 64